C◈MPASS
Catholic Ministries

Your Money Counts

"God's direction for spending, saving, giving, investing and getting out of debt."

Your Money Counts

Published by Compass Catholic Ministries

Copyright © 1996 by Compass—Finances God's Way. All rights reserved. Revisions and New Chapter © 2011 by Howard L. Dayton, Jr. All rights reserved.

Catholic Revisions edited by Jon & Evelyn Bean. Catholic Revisions© 2017 COMPASS Catholic Ministries. All Rights Reserved.

Some of this material previously appeared in Your Money: Frustration or Freedom? Published by Tyndale House Publishers, copyright © 1979 by Howard L. Dayton, Jr.

Scripture texts in this work are taken from the *New American Bible with Revised New Testament and Revised Psalms* © 1991, 1986, 1970 Confraternity of Christian Doctrine, Washington, D.C. and are used by permission of the copyright owner. All Rights Reserved. No part of the New American Bible may be reproduced in any form without permission in writing from the copyright owner.

Scripture quotations marked (GNT) are from the Good News Translation (Catholic Edition) in Today's English Version- Second Edition © 1992 by American Bible Society. Used by Permission.

Scripture quotations marked (RSV CE) are from The Catholic Edition of the Revised Standard Version of the Bible, copyright 1965, 1966 by the Division of Christian Education of the National Council of the Churches of Christ in the United States of America. Used by permission. All rights reserved.

English translation of the Catechism of the Catholic Church for the United States of America Copyright © 1994, United States Catholic Conference, Inc.— Libreria Editrice Vaticana. English translation of the: Catechism of the Catholic Church Modifications from the Editio Typica Copyright © 1997, United States Catholic Conference, Inc. – Libreria Editrice Vaticana. Used with permission.

Excerpts from Stewardship: A Disciple's Response Copyright © 2002 United States Conference of Catholic Bishops, Washington D.C. Used with permission. All rights reserved. No part of this work may be reproduced or transmitted in any form without the permission in writing from the copyright holder.

Excerpts from *United States Catholic Catechism for Adults* Copyright © 2006 United States Conference of Catholic Bishops, Washington D.C. Used with permission. All rights reserved. No part of this work may be reproduced or transmitted in any form without the permission in writing from the copyright holder.

ISBN 978-0-9831331-0-0

Printed in the United States of America

14 13 12 11 10 09
16 15 14 13 12 11

To Bev, my wife,
God's choice gift to our family

To Matthew, my beloved son,
and to Danielle, a joy

To Jim Seneff, without his vision
this book would never have been conceived

To Will Norton, without his skill
this book would never has been born

To Tim Manor, who is closer than a brother,
and George Fooshee, my mentor

To the Compass—Finances God's Way family,
To Jon and Evelyn Bean, founders of Compass Catholic,
for their hearts to serve the Catholic community,
precious co-laborers,
you mean more to me than I can ever say

—HOWARD DAYTON

This book is dedicated to Howard Dayton,
the original author of Your Money Counts.

We are forever grateful to Howard, a godly man,
whose passion for following the Bible in money matters
saved our marriage.

We appreciate all he has done to allow us to edit his
material and present it from a Catholic perspective.

To each of you reading this,
we pray that your interaction with
Compass Catholic Ministries will be one small step
in a long and faith filled life journey.

—JON AND EVELYN BEAN

TABLE OF CONTENTS

ONE

THE PROBLEM

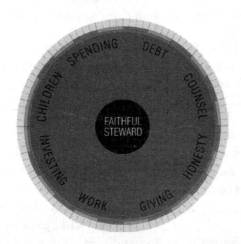

Allen and Jean Hitchcock decided to end their marriage of 24 years.

In anticipation of the divorce settlement, Allen began to review the family's financial records. As he sorted through the files, he came across an old faded check made out to the hotel where he and Jean had stayed on their honeymoon. Another check had paid for an installment on their first car. He picked up still another check and remembered with fatherly pride how he had written it out to the hospital when their daughter was born. And then there was the down payment on their first home . . .

After several hours of sorting through their financial records, Allen realized how much he and his wife had invested in their marriage.

He paused, deep in thought for several minutes. Then he closed the file and dialed his wife's number. After an awkward exchange he blurted out the reason for his call. Would she work with him to rebuild their marriage?

While a family crisis such as Allen and Jean's may be foreign to some of us, the message of their family's finances is common. It is the story of our lives. It tells of our values, how much we save, what we spend, to whom we give. In fact, our bank statements tell us more about our priorities than does anything else.

That's why the Bible says so much about money and possessions. It contains 500 verses on prayer, fewer than 500 verses on faith, but more than 2,500 verses on money and possessions. Fifteen percent of everything Jesus said had to do with it.

The Bible contains 500 verses on prayer, fewer than 500 verses on faith, but more than 2,500 verses on money and possessions.

The Lord said a lot about it because he loves and cares deeply for us. He realizes that from time to time all of us will experience financial challenges, and he wants us to handle money in a way that pleases him and is the smartest way for us. He dealt with money matters because money does matter.

TWO

THE ANSWER

The Bible Is a Compass Giving Us God's Direction for Handling Money

Howard was sliding papers and reports into his briefcase when the phone rang on his desk. It was 5:30 p.m., and he was getting ready to go home after a long day of paperwork and personal conferences. Howard was tired. Reluctantly, he picked up the phone.

"Hello, Howard. This is Allen Hitchcock."

Howard felt a pang of embarrassment. He had neglected to return Allen's earlier call. He sounded depressed, and Howard made a lame apology for not calling him back.

"Jean and I considered a divorce, but we decided to try to work it out," Allen said, his voice sounding strained.

Their financial problems were on the verge of destroying their marriage. Allen asked if he could meet with Howard to discuss their situation. They had become acquainted at church two years before, when they had moved from St. Louis to Orlando. Allen earned a middle-income salary as an assistant manager for a department store, but he couldn't understand where the money went. They faced increasing expenses for their growing family, and in a few years they would need college tuition for the children. Neither he nor Jean could foresee a brighter future.

> *If then you have not been faithful in handling worldly wealth, how can you be trusted with true wealth?*
>
> Luke 16:11 GNT

In addition, the Hitchcocks owed a substantial amount to retail stores, doctors, credit card companies and their bank. They had a sizable home mortgage.

Because of their debts and their increasing daily expenses, the Hitchcocks shopped carefully, sometimes comparing half a dozen outlets for the best price. They used cents-off coupons at the grocery store. Jean avoided buying expensive convenience foods. But the family faced a critical problem. Jean and Allen did not have a clear guideline for handling money. They never had been able to budget their spending. They seldom decided not to buy what they wanted, and they had no plan to save or invest for the future.

Howard understood their predicament. Several years before, Howard and a friend, Jim Seneff, found themselves making daily financial decisions for their expanding businesses and young families without a scriptural point of reference. To be the best husbands and the best businessmen they could be, they felt compelled to do a thorough study of what Scripture said about money. Together Howard and Jim read the entire Bible, locating each of the verses that dealt with money and arranging those verses by topics. Then they put this information into a seminar and presented it at their church. The response was remarkable. People bombarded them with questions and described several areas of intense frustration. Other churches asked for the seminar, and through the years the seminar developed into the Compass Catholic Ministries small group studies, which are today conducted in churches throughout the world.

It is through these small group studies that many people like the Hitchcocks have been helped. We have found that most people—indeed, most Christians—either don't know or have not applied God's financial principles to their lives. Nevertheless, applying these principles is crucial for three reasons.

1. How we handle money affects our relationship with the Lord.

In Luke 16:11 we read, "If, then, you have not been faithful in handling worldly wealth, how can you be trusted with true wealth?" (GNT) In this verse Jesus equates how we handle our money with the quality of our spiritual life. If we handle our money properly according to the principles of Scripture, our relationship with Christ will grow stronger. However, if we manage money unfaithfully, our relationship with him will suffer.

Someone once told me that the Lord often allows a person to teach a subject because he or she desperately needs it. That is certainly true for me in the area of money. I have had the privilege of leading dozens of Compass Catholic small group studies, and I have never met anyone who had more wrong attitudes about money or who handled their finances more contrarily to Scripture than we did. When I learned these principles and applied them, I experienced a dramatic improvement in my relationship with the Lord. Following God's financial principles will draw us closer to Christ.

2. Possessions compete with the Lord.

Possessions are a primary competitor with Christ for lordship of our lives. Jesus tells us we must choose to serve only one of these two masters: "You cannot be a slave of two masters; you will hate one and love the other; you will be loyal to one and despise the other.

You cannot serve both God and money" (Matthew 6:24, GNT). It is impossible for us to serve money—even in a small way—and still serve the Lord.

When the Crusades were being fought during the 12th century, the crusaders employed mercenaries to fight on their behalf. Because it was a religious war, the crusaders insisted that the mercenaries be baptized before fighting. As they were being baptized the mercenaries would hold their swords out of the water to symbolize the one thing in their life that Jesus Christ did not control. They had the freedom to use the swords in any way they wished.

Today many people handle their money in a similar fashion, though they may not be as obvious about it. They hold their wallet or purse "out of the water," in effect saying, "God, You can be the Lord of my entire life except for my money. I am perfectly capable of handling that myself."

3. Much of life revolves around the use of money.

During your normal week, how much time do you spend earning money in your job, making decisions on how to spend money, thinking about where to save and invest money or praying about your giving? Fortunately, God has prepared us adequately for these tasks by giving us the Bible as his blueprint for handling money.

THE ANSWER

Increasingly, people wonder where they can turn for help. There are two basic alternatives: the Bible and the answers people devise. The way most people handle money is in sharp contrast to God's financial principles. Isaiah 55:8 reads, "'For my thoughts are not your thoughts, nor are your ways my ways,' declares the LORD."

To help you recognize the differences between these two ways, a brief comparison appears at the end of each chapter under the heading "Contrast."

LEARNING TO BE CONTENT

Contentment is mentioned six times in the Bible, and five of those refer to money. In Philippians 4:11-13 Paul writes,

"For I have learned . . . to be content . . . in any and all circumstances. I have learned the secret of facing plenty and hunger, abundance and want. I can do all things in him who strengthens me" (RSVCE).

Examine these verses carefully. We are not born with the instinct for contentment; rather, it is learned.

The purpose of this book is to help you learn the biblical principles of handling money and possessions. The book will offer you practical ways to integrate these principles into your life. As you discover these principles and put them into practice, you will draw closer to Christ, submit more fully to him as Lord, learn to be content and set your financial house in order.

CONTRAST

Society says: God plays no role in handling money, and my happiness is based on being able to afford my desired standard of living.

Scripture says: As you learn and follow the scriptural principles of how to handle money, you will draw close to Christ and learn to be content in every circumstance.

THREE

GOD'S PART

The Foundation

On a rainy November morning, Allen and Jean Hitchcock arrived at Howard's office to work through their financial problems in an attempt to save their marriage.

Allen and Jean were Christians, but they had never been exposed to the Bible's perspective on money and possessions. They appreciated their beautiful two-story brick house in suburban Orlando, their two late-model automobiles and their other possessions. Both felt that they had worked hard for what they had and that they had earned the right to enjoy "the good life." However, after financial pressures threatened their standard of living, their lack of contentment surfaced in a major marital crisis. A serious lack of communication existed about their family finances. Allen and Jean each had their own opinions on how to spend the family income, and they had never been able to discuss the subject without ending up in an argument.

They were close to losing everything to their creditors. That, coupled with the possibility of divorce, had jarred them from their complacency. So when Howard sat down with Allen and Jean on the Friday after Thanksgiving, they were motivated to learn what the Bible says about money.

Scripture teaches there are two distinct parts to the handling of money: the part God plays and the part we play. Most of the confusion relating to the handling of money arises from the fact that these two parts are not clearly understood.

God's part is the foundation of contentment. In Scripture God calls himself by more than 250 names. The name that best describes God's part in the area of money is Master. This is the most important chapter of the entire book because how we view God determines how we live. For example, after losing his children and all his possessions, Job was still able to worship God. He knew the Lord and the Lord's role as Master of those possessions. Similarly, Moses forsook the treasures of Egypt and chose to suffer mistreatment with the people of God. Both Job and Moses knew the Lord and accepted his role as Master.

Let's examine what the Bible has to say about God's part in three crucial areas: ownership, control and provision.

> *Everything in heaven and earth is yours, and you are king, supreme ruler over all. All riches and wealth come from you; you rule everything by your strength and power; and you are able to make anyone great and strong.*
>
> (1 Chronicles 29:11-12, GNT)

OWNERSHIP

The Bible clearly states that God is sole owner of everything "The world and all that is in it belong to the LORD; the earth and all who live on it are his" (Psalm 24:1, GNT). Scripture even reveals specific items God owns. Leviticus 25:23 (GNT) identifies him as owner of all the land: "Your land must not be sold on a permanent basis, because you do not own it . . . " Haggai 2:8 (GNT) reveals that "All the silver and gold of the world is mine." And in Psalm 50:10 (GNT), the Lord tells us: ". . . All the animals in the forest are mine and the cattle on thousands of hills."

The Lord is the Creator of all things, and he has never transferred the ownership of his creation to people. In Colossians 1:17 we are told that "in him all things hold together." At this very moment the Lord literally holds everything together by his power. Recognizing God's ownership is critical in allowing Jesus Christ to become the Lord of our money and possessions.

Ownership or Lordship?

If we are going to be genuine followers of Christ, we must transfer the ownership of our possessions to the Lord. ". . . None of you can be my disciple unless you give up everything you have" (Luke 14:33, GNT). In Howard's experience he has found that the Lord will sometimes test us by asking that we be willing to relinquish the very possession that is dearest to us.

Scripture's most vivid example of this is when the Lord told Abraham "Take your son . . . your only son, Isaac, whom you love so much, and . . . offer him as a sacrifice to me . . ." (Genesis 22:2, GNT). When Abraham obeyed, demonstrating his willingness to give up his most prized possession, God provided a substitute ram for the offering, and Isaac was not harmed.

Outstanding author Larry Burkett observed, "When we acknowledge God's ownership, every spending decision becomes a spiritual decision. No longer do we ask, 'Lord, what do you want me to do with my money?' The question is restated, 'Lord, what do you want me to do with your money?'" When we have this perspective, spending and saving decisions are equally as spiritual as giving decisions.

CONTENTMENT

To learn to be content, you must recognize God as the owner of all your possessions. If you believe you own even a single possession, then the circumstances affecting that possession will be reflected in your attitude. If something favorable happens to that possession, then you will be happy. But if something bad occurs, you will be discontented.

After Jim Seneff went through the exercise of transferring ownership of everything he possessed to God, he bought a new car. It was just two days old when a young person drove into the side of it. Jim's first reaction was, "Well, God, I don't know why you want a dent in the side of your new car, but you certainly have a big one!"

Yet it is not easy to maintain this perspective consistently. It is far too easy to think that the possessions we have and the money we earn are entirely the result of our skills and achievements. We find it difficult not to believe we have earned the right to their ownership. I am the master of my fate, the humanist says. I alone own my possessions. Obviously, this view of ownership is the prevailing one in our culture.

Giving up ownership is not easy, nor is it a once-and-for-all transaction. We constantly need to be reminded that God owns all our possessions.

CONTROL

God guides his creation toward its completion or perfection through what we call his Divine Providence. This means that God has absolute sovereignty over all that he has made and guides his creation according to the divine plan of his will. . . . The Father of all continues to work with his Son, who is eternal Wisdom, and with the Holy Spirit, who is the inexhaustible source of life, to guide creation and humanity to the fullness of God's truth, goodness, and beauty. (USCCB, United States catechism for Adults, 56). Examine several of the names of God in Scripture: Master, Almighty, Creator, Shepherd, Lord of lords and King of kings. It's obvious who is in charge:

> Everything in heaven and earth is yours, and you are king, supreme ruler over all. All riches and wealth come from you; you rule everything by your strength and power; and you are able to make anyone great and strong (1 Chronicles 29:11-12, GNT).

Psalm 135:6 (GNT) reads, "He does whatever he wishes in heaven and on earth, in the seas and in the depths below." And in Daniel 4:31-32 King Nebuchadnezzar stated, "I blessed the Most High, I praised and glorified him who lives forever . . . he does as he pleases with the powers of heaven as well as with those who live on the earth. There is no one who can stay his hand or say to him, 'What have you done?'"

The Lord has sovereign control of even difficult circumstances. "I am the LORD and there is no other god. I create both light and darkness; I bring both blessing and disaster. I, the LORD, do all these things" (Isaiah 45:6-7, GNT). In time we can discover that God in his almighty providence can bring a good from the consequences of an evil, even a moral evil, caused by his creatures: "It was not you", said Joseph to his brothers, "who sent me here, but God. . . You meant evil against me; but God meant it for good, to bring it about that many people should be kept alive" (Genesis 45:7-8). From the greatest moral evil ever committed - the rejection and murder of God's only Son, caused by the sins of all men - God, by his grace that "abounded all the more" (CF Romans 5:20), brought the greatest of goods: the glorification of Christ and our redemption. But for all that, evil never becomes a good (CCC 312).

The Lord allows difficult circumstances to enter our lives for at least three reasons: (1) to develop our character, (2) to accomplish his intentions, and (3) to lovingly discipline us when needed. We will examine this in greater detail in Chapter 17 — Crisis.

PROVISION

The third element of God's part is that he has promised to provide our needs "Seek first the kingdom [of God] and his righteousness, and all these things [food and clothing] shall be given to you besides" (Matthew 6:33). The same Lord who fed manna to the children of Israel during their 40 years of wandering in the wilderness, and who satisfied the hunger of 5,000 with only five loaves and two fish, has promised to meet all of our needs. This is the same Lord who told Elijah, "'The brook will supply you with water to drink, and I have commanded ravens to bring you food there'. . . ravens brought him bread and meat every morning and every evening" (1 Kings 17:4, 6, GNT).

God is both predictable and unpredictable. He is absolutely predictable in his faithfulness to provide for our needs. What we cannot predict is how the Lord will provide. He uses various and sometimes surprising means of meeting our needs. He may increase our income, provide a gift or stretch our limited resources through money-saving purchases. Regardless of how he chooses to provide for our needs, he is utterly reliable.

First Timothy 6:8 tells us that our needs are food and covering. In other words, there is a difference between needs and wants. A need is a basic necessity of life—food, clothing or shelter. A want is anything more than a need. A steak dinner, a new car and the latest fashions are all wants.

God's part in helping us reach contentment is that he has obligated himself to provide our needs. However, he has not promised to provide our wants. He promises to provide our needs, and he tells us to· be content when these needs are met. "And if we have food and clothing, we shall be content" (1 Timothy 6:8).

Let me illustrate God's provision with a story.

As World War II was drawing to a close, the Allied armies gathered up many hungry orphans. They were placed in camps where they were well-fed. Despite excellent care, they slept poorly. They seemed nervous and afraid. Finally, a psychologist came up with a solution. Each child was given a piece of bread to hold after he was put to bed. If he was hungry, more food was provided, but when he was finished, this particular piece of bread was just to be held—not eaten.

The piece of bread produced wonderful results. The children went to bed, instinctively knowing they would have food to eat the next day. That guarantee gave the children a restful and contented sleep.[1]

Similarly, the Lord has given us his guarantee—our "piece of bread." As we cling to his promises of provision, we can relax and be content. "And with all his abundant wealth through Christ Jesus, my God will supply all your needs" (Philippians 4:19, GNT). So even if you are in the middle of an extreme financial problem, you can be content because the Lord has promised to feed, clothe and shelter you.

I am convinced that the Lord will provide—at just the right time—the resources necessary for us to fulfill the purpose and calling he has for each of us. This is illustrated in 2 Samuel 12:7-8 (GNT) when he spoke to David through Nathan the prophet: "Thus says the LORD God of Israel: I anointed you king over Israel. I delivered you from the hand of Saul. I gave you your lord's house and your lord's wives for your own. I gave you the house of Israel and of Judah. And if this were not enough, I could count up for you still more."

From the life of David we see that God did not provide all the necessary resources for him to be king all at once. They came at the appropriate time, as David needed them. Occasionally, the Lord has withheld resources from Compass. I sometimes have been confused when this has occurred. Later I discovered that if we had received them too soon, we would not have spent them wisely.

GETTING TO KNOW GOD

The basic reason we fail to recognize God's part is that we do not understand who God is. We often have no genuine awe for the Lord "who stretched out the heavens and laid the foundations of the earth" (Isaiah 51:13). We tend to shrink God down and fit him into a mold with human abilities and limitations. However, we can expand our vision to capture the true perspective of God by studying what the Bible tells us about him. The following is but a sample:

Lord of the Universe

The Lord's power and ability are beyond our understanding. Astronomers estimate that there are more than 100 billion galaxies in the universe, each containing billions of stars. The distance from one end of a galaxy to the other is often measured in millions of light years. Though our sun is a relatively small star, it could contain more than one million earths, and it has temperatures of 20 million degrees at its center. Baruch wrote: ". . . he established the earth for all time . . . the light trembled and obeyed when he called. He sent it forth, and it appeared. He called the stars, and they promptly answered; they took their places and gladly shone to please the one who made them . . . " (Baruch 3:32-34, GNT).

Lord of the Nations

Examine the Lord's role and position relative to nations and people. Isaiah 40:21-23 (GNT) tells us, "Do you not know? . . . . Have you not heard . . . It [the earth] was made by the one who sits on his throne above the earth and beyond the sky; the people below look as tiny as ants . . . He brings down powerful rulers and reduces them to nothing." From Isaiah 40:15, 17 (GNT) we read, "To the LORD the nations are nothing, no more than a drop of water; the distant islands are as light as dust. The nations are nothing at all to him."

Lord of the Individual

God is not an aloof, disinterested "force." Rather, he is intimately involved with each of us as individuals. Psalm 139:3-4, 16 (GNT) reveals "You know all my actions. Even before I speak, you already know what I will say. You saw me before I was born. The days allotted to me had all been recorded in your book, before any of them ever began." The Lord is so involved in our lives that he reassures us, "Even the hairs of your head have all been counted" (Matthew 10:30, GNT). Our heavenly Father is the One who knows us the best and loves us the most.

God hung the stars in space, fashioned the earth's towering mountains and mighty oceans, and determined the destiny of nations. Jeremiah observed correctly, "Nothing is too difficult for you" (Jeremiah 32:17). Yet God knows when a sparrow falls to the ground. He is the Lord of the infinite and the infinitesimal.

In summary, let's review what God's part is. He is the owner, he has sovereign control of every circumstance, and he has promised to meet our needs. In other words, God who created the world and holds it together is able to perform his responsibilities and keep his promises. However, God's part is only half of the equation. It is the most important part, but it is only half. In the next chapter we will begin to examine the other half, our part.

CONTRAST

Society says: What I possess, I alone own; I alone control my destiny.

Scripture says: What I possess, God owns. He is the sovereign, living God who controls all events.

At the end of most chapters, after the CONTRAST between society and Scripture, there will be a COMMITMENT section that will give you the opportunity to practice the biblical principle just covered. We challenge and encourage you to do the COMMITMENT sections because they will help make the principles a part of your life.

COMMITMENT

In the Compass small group study we go through an exercise of transferring the ownership of our possessions to the Lord. We use a deed to do this because a deed is often used to transfer the ownership of property.

When participants in the Compass studies complete and sign the deed, they are acknowledging that God is owner of their assets. The exercise is important because we all occasionally forget that God owns everything. We act as if we own it all. By signing the deed, a person establishes a specific time when God's ownership is acknowledged. Thus, a person can refer to the document repeatedly and recall that God owns everything.

The following will help you complete the deed:

1. Insert today's date.

2. Print your name. You are the one transferring ownership.

3. The Lord is the One receiving the assets.

4. Give prayerful consideration to the possessions you wish to acknowledge God owns. Then list those items.

5. Sign your name.

6. On the lower left-hand corner there is a space for the signature of two witnesses. These friends can help hold you accountable for recognizing God as owner of your possessions.

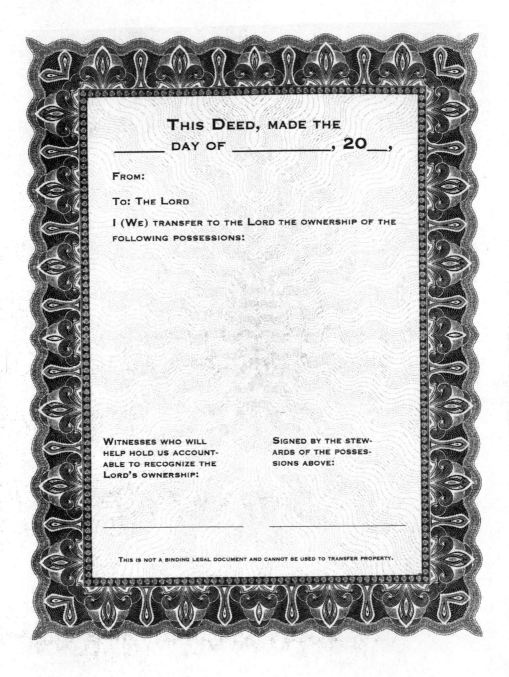

THIS DEED, MADE THE

_____ DAY OF _____, 20___,

FROM:

TO: THE LORD

I (WE) TRANSFER TO THE LORD THE OWNERSHIP OF THE FOLLOWING POSSESSIONS:

WITNESSES WHO WILL HELP HOLD US ACCOUNT-ABLE TO RECOGNIZE THE LORD'S OWNERSHIP:

SIGNED BY THE STEW-ARDS OF THE POSSES-SIONS ABOVE:

_____   _____

THIS IS NOT A BINDING LEGAL DOCUMENT AND CANNOT BE USED TO TRANSFER PROPERTY.

FOUR

OUR PART

Good and Faithful

After he and Jean finished signing the deed, Allen slid it across the desk. "I feel a lot of relief," he said. "But I also feel like I'm supposed to do something." Allen was right. We cannot just sit back, do nothing and wait for God to perform. We have a responsibility. But, like Allen, we may not know exactly what our part is.

God, the Master, is the owner of everything, the controller of all events and our provider. Our responsibility is to be a steward. The word for steward can be translated into two different words: manager and supervisor. In Scripture the position of a steward is one of great responsibility. He or she is the supreme authority under the

21

master and has full responsibility for all the master's possessions and household affairs.

As we examine Scripture we see that God, as Master, has given us the authority to be stewards. "You appointed them rulers over everything you made; you placed them over all creation" (Psalm 8:6, GNT).

FAITHFULNESS

One's only responsibility is to be faithful. "Now it is of course required of stewards, that they be found trustworthy" (1 Corinthians 4:2). Before we can be faithful, we must know what we are required to do. Just as the purchaser of complicated machinery studies the manufacturer's manual to learn how to properly operate it, we need to examine the Creator's handbooks, the Holy Scripture, the Catechism of the Catholic Church, and sacred Tradition—to determine how he wants us to handle his possessions. Several elements of faithfulness are important to understand.

1. Faithful with All Our Resources.

God wants us to be faithful in handling all of our money. Unfortunately, most Catholics have been taught how to handle only some of our income God's way—the area of giving. Although this area is crucial, so is the rest of our income, which we frequently handle from the world's perspective, not from God's perspective.

As a result of not being taught to handle money biblically, many Christians have developed flawed attitudes about possessions. This often causes them to make poor financial decisions—with painful consequences. Hosea 4:6 (GNT) reads, "My people are doomed because they do not acknowledge me." Ignorance of or disobedience to scriptural financial principles frequently causes money problems.

2. Faithful Regardless of How Much We Have.

The issue in Scripture is how to handle faithfully all God has entrusted to us. The faithful steward is responsible for what he or she has, whether it is much or little. The parable of the talents illustrates this. ". . . it will be as when a man who was going on a journey called in his servants and entrusted his possessions to them. To one he gave five talents; to another, two; to a third, one—to each according to his ability" (Matthew 25:14-15).

When the owner returned, he held each one accountable for managing his possessions faithfully. The owner commended the faithful servant who received the five talents: "Well done, my good and faithful servant. Since you were faithful with small matters, I will give you great responsibilities. Come, share your master's joy" (Matthew 25:21).

Interestingly, the servant who had been given two talents received an identical reward as the one who had been given the five talents (see Matthew 25:23). We are required to be faithful whether we are given much or little. In 1 Peter 4:10 we are told, "As each one has received a gift, use it to serve one another as good stewards of God's varied grace."

What identifies a steward? The Catechism provides several answers.

> Safeguarding material and human resources and using them responsibly are one answer; so is generous giving of time, talent, and treasure. But being a Christian steward means more. As Christian stewards, we receive God's gifts gratefully, cultivate them responsibly, share them lovingly in justice with others, and return them with increase to the Lord. (USCCB; *United States Catholic Catechism for Adults;* Washington, D.C. July 2006; 450)

We are required to be faithful whether we are given much or little. As someone once said, "It's not what I would do if a million dollars were my lot; it's what I am doing with the ten dollars I've got."

3. Faithfulness in Little Things.

Luke 16:10 (GNT) reads, "Whoever is faithful in small matters will be faithful in large ones; whoever is dishonest in small matters will be dishonest in large ones." How do you know if a child is going to take good care of his first car? Observe how he cared for his bicycle. How do you know if a salesperson will do a competent job of serving a large client? Observe how she served a small client. If we have the character to be faithful with small things, the Lord knows he can trust us with greater responsibilities.

4. Faithfulness with Another's Possessions.

Faithfulness with another's possessions will, in some measure, determine the amount with which you are entrusted. "If you are not trustworthy with what belongs to another; who will give you what is yours?" (Luke 16:12). This is a principle that is often overlooked. Are you faithful with another's possessions when you are allowed to borrow them? Are you careless with your employer's office supplies? Do you waste electricity when you are staying in a motel room? When someone allows you to use something, are you careful to return it in good shape? I am certain some people have not been given more because they have been unfaithful with the possessions of others.

> *Be faithful in small things because it is in them that your strength lies.*
>
> —Mother Teresa

We need to keep in mind that our role as stewards is all encompassing. "Christian stewardship, therefore, applies to everything—all personal talents, abilities, and wealth; the local, national and worldwide environment; all human and natural resources wherever they are; the economic order; governmental affairs; and even outer space. This stewardship does not tolerate indifference to anything important in God's world" (USCCB, *Stewardship: A Disciple's Response*, 48).

God promises to do his part in our finances. Our part is to grow faithfully as stewards.

5. Faithfulness Builds Character.

God uses money to refine our character. In 1918 David McConaughy wrote a book, *Money, the Acid Test*. In it he said:

> Money, most common of temporal things, involves uncommon

and eternal consequences. Even though it may be done quite unconsciously, money molds people—in the process of getting it, of saving it, of using it, of giving it, of accounting for it. Depending upon how it is handled, it proves a blessing or a curse to its possessor; either the person becomes master of the money, or the money becomes master of the person.

Our Lord takes money, the thing that, essential though it is to our common life, sometimes seems so sordid, and he makes it a touchstone to test the lives of people and an instrument for molding them into the likeness of himself.[2]

We can see correlations between the development of people's character and how they handle money throughout the Bible. Money is regarded as an index of a person's true character. You've no doubt heard the expression, "Money talks," and indeed it does. You can tell a lot about a person's character by examining his or her bank and credit card statements. Why? We spend our money on the things that are most important to us.

6. Faithfulness Leads to Contentment.

Once we know God's part and faithfully do our part, we can be content. In Philippians we discover that Paul has learned to be content because he knew that God would supply all his needs (Philippians 4:19), and he had been faithful. "Keep on doing what you have learned and received and heard and seen in me. Then the God of peace will be with you" (Philippians 4:9).

As we apply the principles of God's economy, we will begin to get out of debt, spend more wisely, start saving for our future goals and give even more to the work of Christ. The Bible offers real solutions to today's financial problems. Each of the following chapters deals with one of the specific areas necessary to equip us to become faithful stewards.

At the beginning of most of the remaining chapters we will complete a section of the "wheel of faithfulness" shown here to help clarify the responsibilities of a faithful steward.

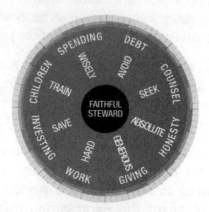

CONTRAST

Society says: You earned your money, now spend it any way you choose and you'll be happy.

Scripture says: You can only be content if you have been a faithful steward handling money from the Lord's perspective.

COMMITMENT

Pray to be a faithful steward of all the blessings that God has provided.

FIVE

DEBT

Act Your Own Wage

The most immediate financial problem facing Allen and Jean was pressure from their creditors. And creditors they had! They had two loans from a bank, bills from three department stores and an outstanding balance on an assortment of credit cards. And then there was the home mortgage.

The Hitchcocks' indebtedness started soon after they had married when they applied for their first loan. Jean, who grew up in a wealthy family, said, "Our friends had new cars, and we felt deprived. We had to have a new car too." Later, when they were transferred to Orlando, they bought a house in the suburbs, borrowing for the down payment. The debts continued to pile up. "Finally," Jean said, "the man from the bank told us he was going to take our house and garnish [take from] Allen's salary."

"Most of our debts were accumulated so slowly through the years," Allen said, "that we didn't realize what was happening until it was too late."

Any government, like any family, can for a year spend a little more than it earns. But you and I know that a continuance of that habit means the poorhouse.

—Franklin D. Roosevelt, 1932

Each year millions of people find themselves in the Hitchcocks' predicament. A credit expert says a major reason is "damage to the borrower's ability to pay." People take out loans on the assumption they will have a steady flow of income; then, the unexpected happens. Someone gets sick. A new baby is on the way. An employer closes shop.

DEBT IS INCREASING

Government, business and personal debt is exploding in our nation. If you converted the total debt to one-dollar bills, placed them end-to-end and pointed them out to space, they would extend more than three billion miles . . . beyond the sun! The economy is riding on a growing mountain of debt.

"With so much credit around you're bound to have casualties," Vern Countryman, a Harvard professor, explains. "It's just like auto accidents. If you're going to have all those cars, you're going to have accidents." In 2010 more than 1.5 million individuals filed for bankruptcy. By 2015 the number of filings was just over .8 million almost a 50 percent reduction from 2010—but still over twice the bankruptcies filed during the Great Depression. Consumers now spend approximately one out of every five dollars in take-home pay on personal debts, not including the home mortgage. More sobering are recent studies that show almost half of those who have stress in a marriage have identified money as the primary stressor. For many, the more accurate marriage vow would have been "till debt do us part." Such financial tension exists largely because consumers believe the "gospel according to Madison Avenue," which says, "Buy now and pay later with easy monthly payments." We all know that nothing about those monthly payments is easy.

WHAT IS DEBT?

Lenders and advertisers use attractive definitions of debt that mask its harsh reality. The Thesaurus lists the following synonyms for debt: liable, minus, owing, in hock, up against it, encumbered, insolvent, in the hole, broke. Do you feel uncomfortable as you read this list? I have yet to see one ad that promises the good life of "buy now and pay later" balanced with these words that describe the reality of debt. Are you beginning to have the feeling that advertisers might not be telling the whole truth of the abundant life as a member of the "debt set"?

The dictionary defines debt as "money or property which one person is obligated to pay to another." Debt includes money owed to credit card companies, bank loans, money borrowed from relatives, the home mortgage and past due medical bills. Bills that come due, such as the monthly electric bill, are not considered debt if they are paid on time.

WHAT DOES DEBT REALLY COST?

We need to understand the real cost of debt. Two common types of debt are credit card debt and the home mortgage.

Credit Card Debt

Assume you have $5,560 in credit card debt at an 18 percent interest rate. This would cost you about $1,000 in interest annually. Study the chart on page 30.

You can see what lenders have known for a long time...compounding interest has an incredible impact. It can work for you, or it can work against you. Assuming that the interest earned or spent has no tax consequences, if you pay a lender $1,000 each year for 40 years, he will accumulate $4,163,213 if he earns 18 percent on your payment. Is there any wonder credit card companies are eager for you to become one of their borrowers?

Now compare the $40,000 you paid in interest during 40 years with the $486,851 you could have accumulated if you had invested $1,000 each year earning 10 percent. Clearly, debt has a much higher cost than many realize. Next time you are tempted to borrow, ask yourself if the long-term benefits of staying out of debt outweigh the short-term benefits of the purchase.

1. Amount of interest you paid:

YEAR 5	YEAR 10	YEAR 20	YEAR 30	YEAR 40
$5,000	$10,000	$20,000	$30,000	$40,000

2. What you would earn on the $1,000 invested at 10 percent:

YEAR 5	YEAR 10	YEAR 20	YEAR 30	YEAR 40
$6,716	$17,531	$63,003	$180,943	$486,851

3. How much the lender earns from your payment at 18 percent:

YEAR 5	YEAR 10	YEAR 20	YEAR 30	YEAR 40
$7,154	$23,521	$146,628	$790,948	$4,163,213

Home Mortgage

A 30-year home mortgage, at a 4.5 percent interest rate, will require you to pay almost twice the amount originally borrowed.

Original mortgage amount $100,000

Monthly mortgage payment at 4.5 percent interest $506.69

Months paid ....x 360

Total payments $182,405

Debt also extracts a physical toll. It often increases stress, which contributes to mental, physical and emotional fatigue. It can stifle creativity and harm relationships. Many people raise their standard of living through debt, only to discover that the burden of debt controls their lifestyles. The bumper sticker that reads, "I owe, I owe, it's off to work I go," is an unfortunate reality for too many people.

WHAT DOES SCRIPTURE SAY ABOUT DEBT?

Scripture's perspective on debt is clear. Read the first portion of Romans 13:8 carefully from several different Bible translations: "Owe no man any thing" (KJV). "Pay all your debts" (TLB). "Owe nothing to anyone" (NAB). "Keep out of debt and owe no man anything" (AMP).

In Proverbs 22:7 we learn why our Lord speaks so directly to the area of debt: "The rich rule over the poor, and the borrower is slave to the lender." When we are in debt, we are in a position of servitude to the lender. Indeed, the deeper we are in debt, the more of a servant we become. We do not have the full freedom to decide where to spend our income because we have legally obligated ourselves to pay our debts.

In 1 Corinthians 7:23 Paul writes, "You were purchased at a price; do not become slaves of human beings." Our Father made the ultimate sacrifice by giving his Son, the Jesus Christ, to die for us. He now wants his children free to serve him in whatever way he chooses.

Debt Considered a Curse

In the Old Testament one of the rewards for obedience was being out of debt "If you continue to heed the voice of the LORD, your God, and are careful to observe all his commandments which I enjoin on you today, the LORD, your God, will raise you high above all the nations of the earth. When you hearken to the voice of the LORD, your God, all these blessings will come upon you... you will lend to many nations and **borrow from none**" (Deuteronomy 28:1-2, 12, emphasis added).

Conversely, indebtedness was one of the curses inflicted for disobedience. "If you do not hearken to the voice of the LORD, your God, and are not careful to observe all his commandments, which I enjoin on you today, all these curses shall come upon you and overwhelm you.... The alien residing among you will rise higher and higher above you, while you sink lower and lower. **He will lend to you**, not you to him. He will become the head, you the tail" (Deuteronomy 28:15, 43-44, emphasis added).

Debt Presumes Upon Tomorrow

When we get into debt, we assume that we will earn enough or will have sufficient resources to pay the debt. We plan for our job to continue or our business or investments to be profitable. Scripture cautions us against presumption "You who say, 'Today or tomorrow we shall go into such and such a town, spend a year there doing business, and make a profit' — you have no idea what your life will be like tomorrow.... Instead you should say, 'If the Lord wills it, we shall live to do this or that'" (James 4:13-15).

Debt May Deny God an Opportunity

The curse and financial bondage of debt is clear when a person is unable to respond when God wants them to do something to build his kingdom. In 1995, we were asked to join the staff of a national ministry to help lead the Catholic initiative. Although we had eliminated some of our debt, we still had too much debt to even think about leaving our jobs.

It was almost twelve years before we were completely debt free and able to begin working for the Lord fulltime. Although we stayed active in the ministry as volunteers, only God knows what we might have accomplished during the twelve years if we had been financially free to join the ministry.

WHEN CAN WE OWE MONEY?

Scripture is silent on the subject of when we can owe money. In my opinion it is possible to owe money for a home mortgage or for your business or vocation. This "possible debt" is permissible, we believe, only if the following three criteria are met.

1. The item purchased is an asset with the potential to appreciate or to produce an income.

2. The value of the item equals or exceeds the amount owed against it.

3. The debt is not so large that repayment puts undue strain on the budget.

Let me give you an example of how a home mortgage might qualify. Historically, the home has usually (but not always as the real estate melt down demonstrated) been an appreciating asset; therefore, it meets the first criterion. Second, if you invest a reasonable down payment of a minimum of at least 20 percent, you could normally expect to sell the home for at least enough to satisfy the mortgage, and this meets the second requirement. Third, the monthly house payment should not strain your budget. As a rule of thumb, all housing expenses (including the mortgage payment, utilities, taxes, insurance, and maintenance) should not exceed 40 percent of your income.

If you meet all the criteria and assume some "possible debt," I hope you will immediately establish the goal of eliminating it. As we've seen, we don't know if the housing market will appreciate or even maintain current values. Moreover, the loss of a job can interrupt your income. Therefore, I urge you to consider prayerfully paying off all debt.

CONTRAST

Society Says: Debt is good.

Scripture Says: Debt is a curse.

COMMITMENT

From today forward incur no new debt.

SIX

GETTING OUT OF DEBT

"D" Day

We have so much personal debt in our nation that the average person has been described as someone driving on a bond-financed highway, in a bank-financed car, fueled by charge-card-financed gasoline, going to purchase furniture on the installment plan to put in his mortgage company-financed home!

"I hope I never pick up another one," Allen said.

"I just didn't know," Jean recalled. "I had no experience."

What were they talking about? Poisonous reptiles? Radioactive material? Hard drugs?

No. Credit cards. The Hitchcocks had run up thousands of dollars of debt on credit cards and were paying a high rate of interest for the "privilege." This is a common predicament. The easy availability of credit has spawned a phenomenal growth in the number of cards held by customers. People hold hundreds of millions of cards, and the average consumer packs away more than six cards in his wallet.

At the end of the initial conference with the Hitchcocks, Allen asked for Howard's scissors. He wanted to perform some "plastic surgery." As a symbol of their vow to get out of debt, he cut their credit cards to ribbons. If they follow through in their commitment, they will be in the minority. Less than 50 percent of those who take the initial step actually follow through and become debt-free.

HOW TO GET OUT OF DEBT

Because of your circumstances, your path for getting out of debt will be unique to you. The following steps are a guide for your journey. The steps are simple, but following them requires hard work. The goal is "D" Day—Debtless Day, the day when you become absolutely free of debt.

1. Pray.

In 2 Kings 4:1-7 a widow was threatened with losing her children to her creditor, and she appealed to Elisha for help. Elisha instructed the widow to borrow many empty jars from her neighbors. The Lord super-naturally multiplied her only possession, a small quantity of oil, and as a result, all the jars were filled. She sold the oil and paid her debts to free her children. The same God who provided for the widow is interested in you becoming free of debt as well.

The first step is the most important. Pray. Ask for the Lord's help and guidance in your journey toward Debtless Day. He might act immediately, as in the case of the widow, or slowly over time. In either case, prayer is essential.

I have observed a trend. As people begin to eliminate debt and accelerate debt repayment, the Lord blesses their faithfulness. Even if you can afford only a small monthly prepayment to reduce your debt, please do it. The Lord can multiply your efforts.

2. Establish a written budget.

In my experience, few people in debt have been using a written budget. They may have had one, neatly filed away in a drawer, but they have not been using it. A written budget helps you plan ahead and analyze your spending patterns to see where you can cut back. It is an effective bridle on impulse spending.

3. List your assets—everything you own.

List every possession you own: your home, car, furniture, etc. Evaluate the list to determine whether you should sell anything. As the Hitchcocks began to consider items they might sell, the most obvious one was their new second car.

"I can't do without my car, Allen," Jean protested.

Allen looked hurt and guilty. He didn't want to deprive his wife of anything she wanted, but they both realized that drastic action was necessary. By deciding to sell the car and Allen's gun collection, the Hitchcocks cut their debt and began to use the amount of the car payment to reduce some of their other debts.

The rich rule over the poor, and the borrower is the slave of the lender.

Proverbs 22:7, RSV CE

While the Catechism does not have any direct references to debt, it does address the issue of wants versus needs that can be summarized in the virtue of temperance. The dictionary definition of temperance is "restraint", "control" and "self-control". Sirach 5:2 helps to define temperance: "Do not follow your inclination and strength, walking according to the desires of your heart." Also in Sirach 18:30 we learn, "Do not follow your base desires, but restrain your appetites" (Cf. CCC1809).

4. List your liabilities—everything you owe.

Many people don't know exactly what they owe. So list your debts to get an accurate picture.

DEBT LIST—WHAT IS OWED

	AMOUNT OWED	MONTHLY PAYMENT	INTEREST RATE
HOME MORTGAGE			
CREDIT CARD COMPANIES			
BANK			
INSTALLMENT LOANS			
LOAN COMPANIES			
INSURANCE COMPANIES			
CREDIT UNION			
LOANS FROM RELATIVES			
SCHOOL LOANS			
BUSINESS LOANS			
MEDICAL BILLS			
OTHERS			
TOTAL DEBTS			

5. Snowball your debt.

Snowball your way out of debt. And here's how. Start with paying off your credit cards because they usually carry the highest interest rate.

In addition to making the minimum payments on all your credit cards, focus on paying off the smallest-balance-card first. You'll be encouraged to see its balance go down, down, and finally disappear!

After the first credit card is paid off, apply its payment toward the next smallest one. After the second card is paid off, apply what you were paying on the first and second toward the third smallest. That's snowball in action!

When you're on a roll like this, it starts getting exciting. Those "impossible" balances that have worried you and robbed you of your peace will begin diminishing before your very eyes.

And after you finish paying off your credit cards, apply the same snowball concept to the rest of your debts—start with the one that has the smallest balance and snowball away!

6. Earn additional income.

Many people hold jobs that simply do not produce enough income to make ends meet and pay off debt even if they spend wisely. Here's what is important about earning additional income. Decide in advance to pay off debts with the added earnings because we tend to spend more than we make, whether we earn a lot or a little.

Jean Hitchcock proved to be an innovative person. She started a "mini-nursery" in her home, babysitting four children from her neighborhood during the day while the children's parents worked. The two older Hitchcock children were also encouraged to babysit in the evenings, and they contributed half of their earnings to the family's debt reduction.

These are only some of the thousands of imaginative ways to earn additional income to get out of debt more quickly. However, no matter how much additional income you earn, the key is a commitment that those moneys be applied to the reduction of debt and not to a higher level of spending.

7. Accumulate no new debt.

The only way I know to accumulate no additional debt is to pay for everything with cash, a check or a debit card at the time of purchase. This raises the issue of credit cards. I don't believe that credit cards are inherently sinful, but they are dangerous. Statistics show that people spend about one-third more when they use credit cards than when they use cash, because they feel they are not really spending money since they are using a plastic card. As one shopper said to another, "I like credit cards a lot more than money because they go so much further!"

When Howard and Bev began this study, they had nine credit cards. Today they carry two. When I analyze the financial situation of people in debt, I use a simple rule of thumb to determine whether credit cards are too dangerous for them. If they do not pay the entire balance due at the end of each month, I encourage them to perform plastic surgery. Any good scissors will do!

8. Be content with what you have.

We live in a culture whose advertising industry has devised powerful, sophisticated methods of persuading the consumer to buy. Frequently the message is intended to create discontentment with what we have.

An American company opened a new plant in Central America because labor was plentiful and inexpensive. The opening of the plant proceeded smoothly until the workers at the plant received their first paychecks. The next day none of the villagers reported for work. Management waited . . . one, two, three days. Still no villagers came to work. The plant manager went to see the village chief to talk about the problem. "Why should we continue to work?" the chief asked in response to the manager's inquiry. "We are satisfied. We have already earned all the money we need to live on."

The plant stood idle for two months until someone came up with the bright idea of sending a mail-order catalog to every villager. Reading the catalogs created new desires for the villagers. Soon they returned to work, and there has been no employment problem since then.

Note these facts:

- The more television you watch, the more you spend.

- The more you look at catalogs and magazines or surf the Web, the more you spend.

- The more you shop, the more you spend.

Howard's family is evidence of this. When his granddaughter suddenly wants a special glass from a fast-food restaurant, he knows she has seen a television commercial. Clearly, limiting our television viewing and Web surfing also limits our wants.

9. Consider a radical change in your lifestyle.

A growing number of people have lowered their expenses significantly to get out of debt more quickly. Some have sold their homes and moved to smaller ones or rented apartments or moved in with family members. Many have sold automobiles with large monthly payments and have purchased inexpensive used cars for cash. They have temporarily lowered their cost of living to become free from debt.

10. Do not give up!

Recognize from the beginning there will be a hundred reasons why you should quit or delay your efforts to get out of debt. Don't yield to the temptation of not following through on your commitment. Don't stop until you have reached the marvelous goal of debt-free living. Remember, getting out of debt is just plain hard work, but the freedom is worth the struggle.

HOW DO WE ESCAPE THE AUTO DEBT TRAP?

Automobile debt is one of the leading causes of consumer indebtedness. About 70 percent of all the cars in our country are financed. The average person keeps a car between three and four years. The average car lasts 10 years.

Here is how you can escape the auto debt trap. First, decide in advance to keep your car for at least three years after you pay off the loan. Second, pay off your auto loan. Third, continue paying the monthly car payment but into your own savings account. Then, when you are ready to replace your car, the saved cash plus the trade-in should be sufficient to buy a good, low-mileage used car without going into debt.

WHAT ABOUT THE HOME MORTGAGE?

I'd like to challenge you to seek the Lord's direction concerning your home mortgage if you own a home. Is it possible that he may want you to pay off everything you owe, including your mortgage? Usually this is a long-term goal because of the size of the average mortgage.

When Howard and Bev began to explore seriously what God wanted for them, they sensed they were to work to pay off everything, including the mortgage. Frankly, this was an unrealistic goal for them at the time, but they researched how this might be accomplished.

Let's examine the payment schedule for a home mortgage. Please don't let the size of the mortgage or the rate of interest hinder your thinking. In the chart that follows we are assuming a $100,000 mortgage at a 4.5 percent interest rate. It is to be paid over 30 years. The first year of the payment schedule (also known as an amortization schedule) would look like the following chart.

As you can see, during the early years of the mortgage almost all the payments go to pay the interest. Of a total $6,080.28 in house payments made during the first year, only $1,613.43 went toward the principal reduction. In fact, it will be about 20 years before the principal and the interest portions of the payment equal each other. I don't know about you, but a 30-year goal to pay off my home mortgage doesn't excite me. If this can be reduced to 15 years, then the goal becomes more attainable.

Payment #	Month	Payment	Interest	Principal	Principal Balance
1	Jan	506.69	375.00	131.69	99,868.31
2	Feb	506.69	374.51	132.18	99,736.17
3	Mar	506.69	374.01	132.67	99,603.46
4	Apr	506.69	373.51	133.17	99,470.29
5	May	506.69	373.01	133.67	99,336.62
6	Jun	506.69	372.51	134.17	99,202.44
7	Jul	506.69	372.01	134.88	99,067.77
8	Aug	506.69	371.50	135.18	98,932.59
9	Sep	506.69	371.00	135.69	98,796.90
10	Oct	506.69	370.49	136.20	98,660.70
11	Nov	506.69	369.98	136.71	98,523.99
12	Dec	506.69	369.46	137.22	98,386.77

Totals for year: 6,080.28   4,466.99   1,613.43

In our example, a $100,000 mortgage at 4.5 percent interest payable over 30 years requires a monthly installment of $506.69 If you increase the monthly payment by $258.30 to $764.99, the mortgage will be fully paid in 15 years and you will have saved $44,710.20 in interest during the life of your mortgage.

Let your lender know what you are planning. Not many borrowers prepay their mortgages, so he may be in shock for a while.

For Bev and Howard, this turned into an exciting time as they began to pay off their mortgage. The Lord provided additional funds in an unexpected way, and today they do not owe anyone anything. Elimination of debt allowed Howard to take time off from his work to study and develop Compass materials. Their living costs are more modest now, because they do not have any debts or house payments. God may have something similar in mind for you.

INVESTMENT DEBT

Should you borrow money to make an investment? I believe it is permissible, but only if you are not personally required to guarantee the repayment of the debt. The investment for which you borrow and any money invested should be the sole collateral for the debt.

As our country has experienced, there are financial events over which you have no control. It is painful to lose your investment, but it is much more serious to jeopardize meeting your needs by risking all your assets on investment debt. This position may appear too conservative; however, many people have lost everything by guaranteeing debt on investments that went sour.

BUSINESS AND PARISH DEBT

I also want to encourage you to pray about becoming debt-free in your business and parish. Many are beginning to pay off all business-related debts, and thousand of parishes are aggressively working toward satisfying their debts.

DEBT REPAYMENT RESPONSIBILITIES

Some people delay payments in order to use the creditor's money as long as possible, but this is not biblical. Proverbs 3:27-28 reads, "Refuse no one the good on which he has a claim when it is in your power to do it for him. Say not to your neighbor, 'Go, and come again, tomorrow I will give,' when you can give at once." Godly people should pay their debts and bills as promptly as they can. We have a policy of trying to pay each bill the same day we receive it to demonstrate to others that knowing Jesus Christ has made us financially responsible.

Should You Use All Your Savings to Pay Off Debt?

In my opinion it is not wise to deplete all your savings to pay off debt.

Maintain a reasonable level of savings to provide for the unexpected. If you apply all your savings against debt and the unexpected does occur, you probably will be forced to incur more debt to fund the emergency.

Bankruptcy

In bankruptcy, a court of law declares a person unable to pay his debts. Depending upon the type of bankruptcy, the court will either allow the debtor to develop a plan to repay his creditors, or the court will distribute his property among the creditors as payment for the debts.

An epidemic of bankruptcy is sweeping our nation. Should a godly person declare bankruptcy? The answer is generally no. Psalm 37:21 tells us, "The wicked borrows and does not pay back . . . ." However, in my opinion, bankruptcy is permissible under two circumstances: a creditor forces a person into bankruptcy, or a counselor believes the debtor's emotional health is at stake because of inability to cope with the pressure of unreasonable creditors. For example, if a husband deserts his wife and children, leaving her with business and family debts for which she is responsible, she may not have the resources or income to meet those obligations. The emotional trauma of an unwanted divorce, coupled with harassment from unsympathetic creditors, may be too much for her to bear.

After a person goes through bankruptcy, he should seek counsel from a competent attorney to determine if it's legally permissible to repay the debt, even though he is not obligated to do so. If it is allowable, he should make every effort to repay the debt. For a large debt, this may be a long-term goal that is largely dependent upon the Lord supernaturally providing the resources.

Cosigning

Related to debt is the matter of cosigning. A person who cosigns becomes legally responsible for the debt of another. It is just as if you went to the bank, borrowed the money and gave it to your friend or relative who is asking you to cosign.

A study by the Federal Trade Commission found that 50 percent of those who cosigned for bank loans ended up making payments. And 75 percent of those who cosigned for finance company loans ended up making payments. Unfortunately, few cosigners plan for default. The casualty rate is so high because the professional lender has analyzed the loan and said to himself, "I won't touch this with a 10-foot pole unless I can get someone who is financially responsible to guarantee this loan."

Fortunately, Scripture speaks very clearly about cosigning. Proverbs 17:18 reads "Senseless is the man who gives his hand in pledge, who becomes surety for his neighbor." The word "senseless" describes the mentality of someone who cosigns. Sirach 29:17 adds that "Going surety has ruined many prosperous men and tossed them about like waves of the sea."

A parent often cosigns for his or her child's first automobile, but we have decided not to do this. We want to model for our children the importance of not cosigning, and we also want to discourage them from using debt. Instead, we trained them to plan ahead and save for the cash purchase of their first car.

I urge you to use sound judgment and never cosign a note or become surety for any debt.

If you have cosigned, Scripture gives you very direct counsel. Proverbs 6:1-5 reads,

> My son, if you have become surety to your neighbor, given your hand in pledge to another, You have been snared by the utterance of your lips, caught by the words of your mouth; So do this, my son, to free yourself, since you have fallen into your neighbor's power: Go, hurry, rouse your neighbor! Give no sleep to your eyes, nor slumber to your eyelids; Free yourself as a gazelle from the snare, or as a bird from the hand of the fowler.

CONTRAST

Society says: You may use debt as often as you wish; buy now and pay later.

Scripture says: The Lord discourages the use of debt because he wants us free to serve him.

COMMITMENT

Formalize your desire to get out of debt. Then follow the 10 steps to becoming debt-free. Seek the help and counsel of some friends who can hold you accountable to stick to your plan.

The value of seeking advice is the subject of the next chapter.

HELPFUL RESOURCE

Free and Clear: God's Road Map to Debt Free Living by Howard Dayton is a very practical book that has helped many make progress of their journey to become free of debt.

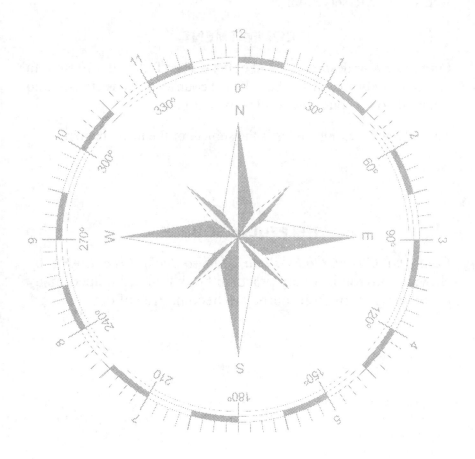

SEVEN

COUNSEL

A Triple-Braided Cord

Jean and Allen were faced with an uncomfortable decision.

Jean's brother and his wife had just moved to Florida from Chicago. Because they experienced financial difficulties in Chicago, the bank would not loan them the money to purchase a home unless they had someone to cosign the note. They asked Allen and Jean to cosign. Jean pleaded for Allen to do so; however, he was reluctant.

When they came asking for advice to resolve this problem, Howard asked them to read the verses from the Bible that addressed cosigning. When Jean read the passages she responded, "Who am I to argue with God? We shouldn't cosign." Allen was relieved.

Two years later, Jean's brother and his wife were divorced and he declared bankruptcy. Can you imagine the strain on Jean and Allen's marriage if they had cosigned that note? They would not have been able to survive financially.

Fortunately, they sought counsel. This is a sharp contrast to our culture's practice that says, be a rugged individualist who makes decisions alone and unafraid, coping with any financial pressure in stoic silence.

King Solomon dominated the world scene in his time. Known as the first great commercial king of Israel, he was a skilled diplomat and director of extensive building, shipping and mining ventures. However, Solomon is most often remembered as the wisest king who ever lived. In fact, he made wisdom a subject of study. In Proverbs he wrote, "I am Wisdom, I am better than jewels; nothing you want can compare with me" (8:11, GNT). Solomon's practical recommendations for embracing wisdom are also found in Proverbs: "Listen to counsel and receive instruction that you may eventually become wise" (19:20). "The way of a fool seems right in his own eyes, but he who listens to advice is wise" (12:15).

WHERE SHOULD WE SEEK COUNSEL?

The Bible encourages us to seek counsel from several sources.

Scripture

The psalmist wrote, "Your instructions give me pleasure; they are my advisers" (Psalm 119:24, GNT). Moreover, the Bible makes this remarkable claim about itself: "The Word of God is living and effective, sharper than any two-edged sword . . . and able to discern reflections and thoughts of the heart" (Hebrews 4:12). You may have been surprised to learn that the Bible contains 2,500 verses dealing with how we should handle money and possessions. The fact is, the Scriptures are the very first filter through which we should run our financial decisions. If the Bible answers the question, we don't have to go any further, because it contains the Lord's written, revealed will.

If the Bible provides clear direction in a financial matter, we know what to do. If the Bible is not specific about an issue, we should subject our decision to additional sources of counsel: the Cathechism, Church teaching and godly people.

Catechism and Church Teaching

"The Cathechism of the Catholic Church is a statement of the Church's faith and of catholic doctrine, attested to or illumined by Sacred Scripture, the Apostolic tradition, and the Church's Magesterium (USCCB, *Cathechism of the Catholic Church*, 3).

"The Cathechism presents the fundamental contents of Catholic doctrine, as regards both faith and morals, in light of the Second Vatican Council and the whole of the Church's Tradition" (CCC, 11). If you are uncertain of the direction you should proceed after reading the Scriptures, the Catechism should be your next point of reference.

Godly People

"The words of good people are wise, and they are always fair. They keep the law of their God in their hearts and never depart from it" (Psalm 37:30-31, GNT). The apostle Paul recognized the benefit of godly counsel. After he was converted on the Damascus road, he never was alone in his public ministry. Paul knew and appreciated the value of a couple of extra sets of eyes looking down that straight and narrow road. Timothy, Barnabas, Luke or someone else was always with him.

In fact, in the New Testament the word *saint* is never used in the singular. It is always in the plural. Someone has described the Christian life as not one of independence from each other but of dependence upon each other. Nowhere is this more clearly illustrated than in Paul's discussion concerning the body of Christ in the 12th chapter of 1 Corinthians. Each of us is pictured as a different part of this body. Our ability to function effectively is dependent upon members working together. In other words, to operate in an optimal way, we need other people to help us. God has given each individual certain abilities and gifts. But God has not given any one person all the skills he or she needs to be most productive.

1. Spouse.

If you are married, your spouse is to be your primary source of human counsel. A husband and wife are one. Women tend to be gifted with a wonderfully sensitive and intuitive nature that usually is very accurate. Men tend to focus objectively on the facts. A husband and wife need each other to achieve the proper balance for a correct decision. I also believe the Lord honors a wife's "office" as helpmate to her husband. Many times the Lord communicates most clearly to a husband through his wife.

Husbands, let's be blunt. Regardless of her business background or her financial aptitude, you must cultivate and seek your wife's counsel. Even though Bev's formal education was not related to business, she has developed excellent business sense, and her decisions are often better than Howard's. Indeed, her perspective always enriches his.

By consistently asking for her advice, you keep your wife informed of your true financial condition. This is important in the event a husband dies before his wife or if he is unable to work. Howard's father suffered a massive heart attack that incapacitated him for two years. Because he had been faithful in keeping Howard's mother abreast of his business, she was able to step in and operate it successfully.

Seeking the counsel of your spouse also helps preserve your relationship because you will both experience the consequences of a decision. If you both agree about a decision, even if it proves to be disastrous, your relationship is more likely to remain intact.

2. Parents.

We should seek counsel of our parents also. Proverbs 6:20-23 (GNT) says, "Son, do what your father tells you and never forget what your mother taught you. Keep their words with you always, locked in your heart. Their teaching will lead you when you travel, protect you at night, and advise you during the day. Their instructions are a shining light; their correction can teach you how to live." Our parents have the benefit of years of experience. They know us so very well, and they have our best interests at heart.

We should seek our parents counsel even if they are not church goers or have not been faithful money managers themselves. It is not uncommon for an unspoken barrier to be erected between a child and his parents. Asking their advice is a way to honor them and to build a bridge across any wall.

Even though obedience to your parents ends when you leave home, respect for your parents should never end. "He who reveres his father will live a long life; he obeys the LORD who brings comfort to his mother. He who fears the LORD honors his father, and serves his parents as rulers. In word and deed honor your father that his blessing may come upon you" (Sirach 3:6-8) (Cf. CCC 2217).

One word of caution, however. Although the husband and wife should seek the counsel of their parents, the advice of the parents should be subordinate to the advice of the spouse—especially if a family conflict materializes.

The Lord

During the process of searching the Bible, Catechism and obtaining the counsel of godly people, we need to ask the Lord for direction. In Isaiah 9:5 we are told that one of the Lord's names is "Wonderful Counselor." The Psalms also identify the Lord as our counselor. "The LORD says, 'I will teach you the way you should go; I will instruct you and advise you'" (Psalm 32:8, GNT). "You guide me with your instruction and at the end you will receive me with honor" (Psalm 73:24, GNT).

We receive the counsel of the Lord by praying and listening. Tell the Lord about your concerns and need for specific direction. Then quietly listen for his still, small voice.

A MULTITUDE OF COUNSELORS

We should try to obtain advice from a multitude of counselors. Proverbs 15:22 reads, "Plans fail when there is no counsel, but they succeed when advisors are many." And Proverbs 11:14 says, "For lack of guidance a people falls; security lies in many counselors."

The older Howard has become and the larger Compass has grown, the more he recognizes the need for a multitude of counselors. Each of us has a limited range of knowledge and experience, and we need others, with their own unique backgrounds, to give us insights and alternatives we never would have considered without their advice.

Another practical way of applying the principle of many counselors is to become involved in a small group. For years I have met regularly with a small group to pray and share. Through the years our group has been through traumatic times together. Newborn babies, deaths of parents, job changes, serious illnesses, starting new businesses, home and financial pressures have marked the years. The advice of these friends has not only benefited our finances but has significantly contributed to our emotional and spiritual health. We have rejoiced together during each other's successes. We have comforted and wept with each other during the difficult times.

We have learned that when someone is subjected to a painful circumstance, it is difficult for him or her to make wise, objective decisions. We have experienced the safety of having a group of people who love one another—even when it hurts. I am more receptive to constructive criticism when it comes from someone I respect, someone who cares for me. Solomon describes the benefits of dependence upon on another in one of my favorite passages.

> Two are better off than one, because together they can work more effectively. If one of them falls down, the other can help him up. But if someone is alone and falls, it's just too bad, because there is no one to help him . . . Two people can resist an attack that would defeat one person alone. A rope made of three cords is hard to break (Ecclesiastes 4:9-10, 12, GNT).

When seeking a multitude of counselors, don't expect them all to offer the same recommendations. They may even disagree sharply, but a common thread usually develops. At other times, each counselor may supply a different insight you need to help you make the decision. We encourage you to include your priest among your counselors, particularly when you face a major crossroads.

BIG DECISIONS

Because of their importance and permanence, some decisions deserve more attention than others. Decisions concerning a career change or a home purchase, for example, affect us for a longer period of time than most other choices we make. Throughout the Bible we are admonished to wait upon the Lord. Whenever you face a major decision or experience a sense of confusion concerning a course of action, We encourage you to set aside some time to pray, fast and listen quietly for his will.

COUNSEL TO BE AVOIDED

We need to avoid one particular source of counsel. "Blessed is the man who does not walk in the counsel of the wicked" (Psalm 1:1). The word "blessed" literally means "happy many times over." A "wicked" person is one who lives his life without regard to God. We can seek specific technical assistance, such as legal and accounting advice, from those who do not know God. Then armed with the technical data, our final decision should be based on the counsel of those who know the Lord.

Never Seek the Counsel of Fortune Tellers or Mediums

The Bible clearly forbids seeking the advice of fortune tellers, mediums, or spiritualists: "Do not go to mediums or consult fortune tellers, for you will be defiled by them. I, the LORD, am your God" (Leviticus 19:31). Study this next passage carefully: "Saul died because he was unfaithful to the LORD. He disobeyed the LORD's commands; he tried to find guidance by consulting the spirits of the dead instead of consulting the LORD. So the LORD killed him and gave control of the kingdom to David son of Jesse" (1 Chronicles 10:13-14, GNT). Saul died, in part, because he went to a sorcerer. We should also avoid anything they use in forecasting the future, such as horoscopes and all other practices of the occult.

Be Careful of the Biased

We need to be cautious of the counsel of the biased. When receiving financial advice, ask yourself this question: What stake does this person have in the outcome of my decision? If the adviser will profit, always seek a second, unbiased opinion.

CONTRAST

Society says: Be your own person; stand on your own two feet. You don't need anyone to tell you what to do.

Scripture says: "Sensible people accept good advice. People who talk foolishly will come to ruin" (Proverbs 10:8, GNT).

COMMITMENT

In our experience, the vast majority of those in financial difficulties have not followed the principle of seeking wise counsel. They have been molded by our culture's view that admitting a need and asking for advice is only for those who are not strong enough to be self-sufficient.

More often than not, a person's pride is the biggest deterrent to seeking advice. This is especially true in a financial crisis. It is embarrassing to expose our problems to someone else.

Another reason for reluctance to seek counsel is the fear that an objective evaluation of our finances may bring to the surface issues we would rather avoid: a lack of disciplined spending, an unrealistic budget, a lack of communication in the family or a suggestion to give up something dear to us.

We cannot overemphasize the importance of counsel, and we encourage you to evaluate your situation. If you do not have a counselor, try to cultivate a friendship with at least one godly person who can advise you.

EIGHT

HONESTY

Absolutely

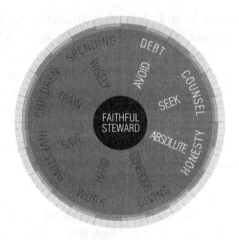

One evening Howard received a phone call he will never forget. It was from Allen Hitchcock. "You won't believe what just happened to me!" he said. "I went to my local gas station and pumped $20 worth of gas. When I asked for a receipt, the attendant made the receipt for $25. When I pointed out this mistake, the attendant replied, 'Oh, just turn in the receipt to your company, and you'll make a fast five bucks. After all, a lot of the mailmen do that.'"

Like Allen, all of us—the executive, the employee and the homemaker— have to make daily decisions about whether or not to handle money honestly. Do you tell the cashier at the grocery store when you receive too much change? Have you ever tried to sell something and been tempted not to tell the whole truth because you might lose a sale?

HONESTY IN SOCIETY

These decisions are made more difficult because everyone around us seems to be dishonest. For example, employee theft in the workplace is approaching $1 billion a week.

Byron was reading the morning paper while his wife, Peggy, prepared breakfast. "Well, would you look at this. Another politician got caught with his hand in the cookie jar," he said. "I'll bet there isn't an honest one in the entire country. What a bunch of crooks!"

Just a few moments later Byron was smirking as he told Peggy how he planned to pad his expense account in such a way that he would get more money from his employer than he was entitled to receive. Byron was not aware of the incongruity between his own behavior and his disgust with dishonesty in others. As he told Peggy, "The way the economy is going, you've got to be shrewd just to survive. The company doesn't need it, and besides, everyone does it."

... everyone did what was right in their own eyes.

Judges 17:6

We live in an age of "relative honesty" in which people formulate their own standards of honesty which change with the circumstances. The Bible speaks of a similar time which was a turbulent period in Israel's history. "In those days there was no king in Israel; everyone did what was right in their own eyes" (Judges 17:6).

HONESTY IN THE BIBLE

Relative honesty contrasts sharply with the standard we find in Scripture. God demands absolute honesty. Proverbs 20:23 reads, "Varying weights are an abomination to the LORD, and false scales are not good." And Proverbs 12:22 states, "Lying lips are an abomination to the LORD." Leviticus 19:11 says, "You shall not steal. You shall not deceive, or speak falsely to one another."

Study this comparison between what the Scriptures teach and what our society practices concerning honesty.

Issue	Scripture	Society
Standard of honesty	Absolute	Relative
God's concern about honesty	He demands honesty	There is no God
The decision to be honest or dishonest is based upon	Faith in the invisible, living God	Only the facts that can be seen
Question usually asked deciding whether to be honest	Will it please God?	Will I get away with it?

The God of Truth

Truthfulness is one of God's attributes. He is repeatedly identified as the God of truth. Jesus said, "I am . . . the truth" (John 14:6, GNT). Our loving heavenly Father commands us to reflect his honest and holy character: "Instead, be holy in all that you do, just as God who called you is holy. The Scripture says, 'Be holy because I am holy'" (1 Peter 1:15-16, GNT). 1 John 1:6 (GNT) adds that, "If, then, we say that we have fellowship with him, yet at the same time live in the darkness, we are lying both in our words and in our actions" (Cf. CCC 2470).

In contrast to God's nature, John 8:44 (GNT) describes the devil's character: ". . . From the very beginning he [the devil] was a murderer and has never been on the side of truth, because there is no truth in him. When he tells a lie, he is only doing what is natural to him, because he is a liar and the father of all lies." The Lord wants us to conform to his honest character rather than to the dishonest nature of the devil (Cf. CCC 2482).

WHY DOES GOD DEMAND ABSOLUTE HONESTY?

God has imposed the standard of absolute honesty for five reasons.

1. We cannot practice dishonesty and love God.

When we practice dishonesty, we are acting as if the living God does not exist, and it is impossible to love God if he doesn't exist. Stop and think about what we are saying when we make a decision to be dishonest:

- God is not able to provide exactly what I need—even though he has promised to do so (Matthew 6:33). I will take things into my own hands and do them my own dishonest way.

- God is incapable of discovering my dishonesty.

- God is powerless to discipline me.

If we really believed that God would discipline us, then we would not consider acting dishonestly.

Honest behavior is an issue of faith. An honest decision may look foolish in light of the circumstances we can observe. However, a godly person has mastered the art of considering another factor which is valid, even though invisible: the person of Jesus Christ. Every honest decision strengthens our faith in the living God. However, if we choose to be dishonest, we essentially deny the existence of the Lord. The Bible declares that those who practice dishonesty hate God: "He who walks uprightly fears the LORD, but he who is devious in his ways spurns him" (Proverbs 14:2).

2. We cannot practice dishonesty and love our neighbor.

The Lord requires honesty because dishonest behavior also violates what Jesus says in Mark 12:31 (GNT), "Love your neighbor as you love yourself." Paul tells the Romans, "Love your neighbor as you love yourself. If you love others, you will never do them wrong . . ." (Romans 13:9-10, GNT; Cf. CCC 2477-2478).

When we act dishonestly, what we're really doing is stealing from another person. We may rationalize that it's a business or the government or an insurance company that is suffering the loss. Yet, if we look at the bottom line, it is the business owners or fellow taxpayers or policyholders from whom we are stealing. It's just as if we took the money from their wallets. In the final analysis, the victim is always a person (Cf. USCCB, *United States Catholic Catechism for Adults*, 419; CCC 2409).

3. Honesty creates credibility for evangelization.

Our Lord demands that we be absolutely honest in order to demonstrate the reality of Jesus Christ to those who do not yet know him. Our actions speak louder than our words. Scripture says "Do everything without complaining or arguing, so that you may be innocent and pure as God's perfect children, who live in a world of corrupt and sinful people. You must shine among them like stars lighting up the sky" (Philippians 2:14-15, GNT).

Robert Newsome had been trying to sell an old pickup truck for months. Finally, an interested buyer decided to purchase the truck, but at the last moment he told Robert, "I'll buy the truck only if you don't report it to the state so I won't have to pay sales tax."

Robert was tempted, but he knew it would be wrong. He responded, "I'm sorry, I can't do that because it's not Scriptural. That's not what Jesus teaches."

"You should have seen the buyer's face," Robert said a few days later. "He almost went into shock. Then an interesting thing happened. He purchased the truck, and his attitude completely changed. He became very open to the truth of knowing Jesus Christ in a personal way." Honest behavior confirms to those who do not yet know him that we serve a holy God.

4. Honesty confirms God's direction.

Proverbs 4:24-26 (GNT) reads, "Never say anything that isn't true. Have nothing to do with lies and misleading words. Look straight ahead with honest confidence; don't hang your head in shame. Plan carefully what you do, and whatever you do will turn out right."

What a tremendous principle! As you are absolutely honest, "whatever you do will turn out right." Choosing to walk the narrow path of honesty eliminates the many possible avenues of dishonesty. Decision-making becomes simpler because the honest path is a clear path.

"If only I'd understood this," Jon thought, I wish I had been more honest.

Evelyn and I wanted that house so much and we thought that we deserved it. It was our dream home, but I was planning on quitting my full time job to begin a new business as soon as the mortgage was in place. I knew that the mortgage company would not qualify us for the mortgage if they were aware of this, so we didn't tell them. That was a terrible decision! Two weeks after we secured the mortgage I quit my job and started the business, but our income was cut by over 60% since there was no money coming from my new business. While we didn't miss any payments, we were digging deeply into our savings and the pressure began to build as we approached the end of that first year.

Then Evelyn was offered a job transfer to Orlando. She was pretty fed up with our situation and told me, "I'm going to Orlando and you can come if you want." What an eye opener for me! Since my marriage was more important than the house or business, I swallowed my pride and told her that I was coming to Orlando. After all, I thought I could start fresh in a new city.

If we had been totally honest, the lender would not have approved the loan. We would not have been able to purchase that particular home. If we had prayed and waited, perhaps the Lord would have helped me to calm my pride and ego and allowed us to purchase something more affordable, thus avoiding the pressure that almost ended our marriage. Honesty helps confirm God's direction.

5. Even the small act of dishonesty is devastating.

God requires us to be absolutely honest because even the smallest act of dishonesty is sin. Even the smallest "white lie" can harden our hearts and make our consciences increasingly insensitive to sin. This can deafen our ears to the still, small voice of the Lord. A single cancer cell of small dishonesty can multiply and spread to greater dishonesty. "Whoever is dishonest in small matters will be dishonest in large ones" (Luke 16-10, GNT).

An event in Abraham's life has challenged me to be honest in small matters. The king of Sodom offered Abraham all the goods Abraham recovered when he returned from successfully rescuing the people of Sodom. Abraham answered the king, "I solemnly swear before the LORD, the Most High God, maker of heaven and earth, that I will not keep anything of yours, not even a thread or a sandal strap" (Genesis 14:22-23, GNT).

Just as Abraham was unwilling to take so much as a thread or a sandal strap, we challenge you to make a similar commitment in this area of honesty. Promise (or make a covenant) not to steal a stamp, or a photocopy, or a paper clip, or a penny from your employer, the government or anyone else.

The people of God must be honest in even the smallest, seemingly inconsequential matters.

HOW DO WE ESCAPE THE TEMPTATION OF DISHONESTY?

Unless we deny ourselves and live our lives yielded to the Holy Spirit, all of us will be dishonest. "Let the Spirit direct your lives, and you will not satisfy the desires of the human nature. For what our human nature wants is opposed to what the Spirit wants, and what the Spirit wants is opposed to what our human nature wants. These two are enemies, and this means that you cannot do what you want to do" (Galatians 5:16-17, GNT). The desire of our human nature is to act dishonestly. "From within people, from their hearts, come evil thoughts . . . theft, murder . . . greed, malice, deceit . . ." (Mark 7:21-22). The desire of the Spirit is for us to be absolutely honest. We can't overemphasize that the life of absolute honesty is supernatural. We must submit ourselves entirely to Christ as Lord and allow him to live his life through us. We heartily recommend a short book by Mother Teresa titled *No Greater Love*. It's an excellent study on yielding fully to Christ.

By a Healthy Fear of the Lord

When we talk of a "healthy fear" of the Lord, we're not implying that God is a big bully just waiting for the opportunity to punish us. Far from it. In fact, he is a loving Father who, out of infinite love, disciplines his children for their benefit. ". . . God does it for our own good, so that we may share his holiness" (Hebrews 12:10, GNT).

Howard once shared a motel room with a friend during a business trip. As they were leaving, the friend slipped one of the motel's drinking glasses into his pocket and walked to the car. Suddenly Howard was overwhelmed by the fear of the Lord. It is difficult to explain the feeling. The closest description he's found is in Daniel 5:6, which records the Babylonian king's reaction to the handwriting on the wall: " . . . his face became pale; his thoughts terrified him, his hip joints shook, and his knees knocked."

There was Howard, with his knees knocking as he thought of Hebrews 12:11, "all discipline seems a cause not for joy but for pain." Discipline hurts! Given the choice, Howard would rather "share his holiness" out of obedience to his Word than to make a deliberate decision that would prompt our loving Father to discipline him. Howard can't tell you how relieved he was when his friend returned the glass after he pleaded with him to do so!

By a Loss of Property

We believe that our heavenly Father will not allow us to keep anything we have acquired dishonestly. Proverbs 13:11 reads, "Wealth quickly gotten dwindles away."

Linda purchased four azalea plants, but the checkout clerk had only charged her for one. She knew it, but she left the store anyway without paying for the other three. She said it was simply miraculous how quickly three of those four plants died.

Think about this for a moment: If you are a parent and your child steals something, do you allow the child to keep it? Of course not. You require its return because the child's character would be damaged if he kept the stolen property. Not only do you insist upon its return, but you probably want the child to experience enough discomfort to produce a lasting impression. For example, you might have the child confess the theft and ask forgiveness from the store manager. When our heavenly Father lovingly disciplines us, it usually is done in such a way that we will not forget.

WHAT SHOULD WE DO WHEN WE HAVE BEEN DISHONEST?

Unfortunately, all of us are dishonest from time to time. Once we recognize that we have acted dishonestly, we need to do three things:

1. Restore our relationship with God.

"I am writing this to you, my children, so that you will not sin; but if anyone does sin, we have someone who pleads with the Father on our behalf—Jesus Christ, the righteous one. And Christ himself is the means by which our sins are forgiven, and not our sins only, but also the sins of everyone" (1 John 2:1-2, GNT). Anytime we sin, we harm our relationship with God and need to restore it. As Catholics, we have the opportunity to "convert and recover the grace of justification through the Sacrament of Penance" (CCC 1446).

2. Restore our relationship with people.

After our relationship with God has been restored, we need to confess our dishonesty to the person we offended. "So then, confess your sins to one another and pray for one another, so that you will be healed" (James 5:16, GNT).

Failing to confess and restore your relationship may result in a lack of financial prosperity. "You will never succeed in life if you try to hide your sins. Confess them and give them up; then God will show mercy to you" (Proverbs 28:13, GNT).

3. Restore any dishonestly acquired property.

If we have acquired anything dishonestly, we must return it to its rightful owner. "If someone commits a sin of dishonesty against the LORD . . . he shall, since he has incurred guilt by his sin, restore the thing that was stolen or unjustly retained . . . or whatever else the he swore falsely about; he shall make full restitution of the thing itself, and in addition, give the owner one fifth of its value to it" (Leviticus 5:21-24; Cf. CCC 2454).

Restitution is a tangible expression of repentance and an effort to correct a wrong. If it's not possible for restitution to be made to the injured party, then the property should be given to the Lord. Numbers 5:8 teaches, ". . . if there is no next of kin, one to whom restitution can be made, the restitution shall be made to the LORD and shall fall to the priest."

BRIBES

A bribe is defined as anything given to a person to influence him to do something illegal or wrong. Taking a bribe is clearly prohibited by Scripture: "Do not accept a bribe, for a bribe makes people blind to what is right and ruins the cause of those who are innocent" (Exodus 23:8 GNT). Bribes are sometimes subtly disguised as a "gift" or "referral fee." Evaluate any such offer to confirm that it is not in reality a bribe.

BLESSINGS AND CURSES

Listed below are some of the blessings the Lord has promised for the honest and some of the curses reserved for the dishonest. Read these slowly and prayerfully and ask God to use his Word to motivate you to a life of honesty.

Blessings Promised for the Honest

- **Intimacy with the Lord.** "To the LORD . . . the upright are close to him" (Proverbs 3:32).

- **A blessed family.** "The just walk in integrity; happy are their children after them!" (Proverbs 20:7).

- **Long life.** "Truthful lips endure forever, the lying tongue, for only a moment" (Proverbs 12:19).

- **Prosperity.** "In the house of the just there are ample resources, but the harvest of the wicked is in peril" (Proverbs 15:6).

Curses Reserved for the Dishonest

- **Alienation from God.** "To the LORD the devious are an abomination . . . " (Proverbs 3:32).

- **Family problems.** "Try to make a profit dishonestly, and you get your family in trouble . . . " (Proverbs 15:27 GNT).

- **Death**. "The riches you get by dishonesty soon disappear, but not before they lead you into the jaws of death" (Proverbs 21:6 GNT).

ARE YOU THE PERSON THE LORD IS LOOKING FOR?

We seriously underestimate the impact that one honest person can have. Read Jeremiah 5:1 carefully: "Roam the streets of Jerusalem, look about and observe . . . find even one who acts justly and seeks honesty, and I will pardon her!" The destiny of an entire city hung in the balance. Its future depended upon there being one absolutely honest person. Will you be that person for your community? You may not receive the acclaim of the media, the business community or politicians, but in God's economy, your commitment to honesty can have a massive influence on your city.

CONTRAST

Society says: You can be dishonest because everyone else is.

Scripture says: The Lord demands absolute honesty in even the smallest matters.

COMMITMENT

Prayerfully review this checklist for honest behavior:

1. Do I report all income on my tax returns, and are all my tax deductions legitimate?

2. Do I care for the property of others as if it were my own?

3. Do I have the habit of telling "little white lies"?

4. Do I ever misappropriate office supplies, stamps or anything else that belongs to my employer?

5. If I am undercharged on a purchase, do I report it?

6. Do I look out for the interests of others as well as my own?

Ask God to show you any other dishonest behavior that should be changed, especially in the gray areas. Ask a close friend to encourage you and to hold you accountable to be honest.

NINE

GIVING

What Is Your Attitude?

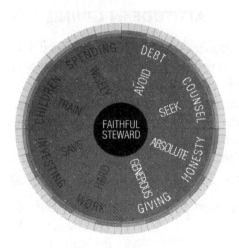

Allen and Jean decided to enroll in a Compass small group study to learn what the Bible teaches about money. A few weeks after the group started, Howard met Allen for breakfast. He told Howard how much the study meant to him, and then sheepishly confessed, "I've never had any desire to give money. Now that I understand what the Bible has to say about it, I want to give, but I'm frustrated. How can I possibly decide where to give? It seems as if my mailbox is constantly filled with appeals. There are so many needs. I feel guilty that perhaps we're not giving enough. And sometimes I become cynical because I feel I'm manipulated subtly by people whose goals may be worthwhile but whose means of achieving those goals are questionable."

Howard knew what Allen was experiencing. He used to be as frustrated as Allen was. Since learning what the Bible says about giving, the Holy Spirit has been changing Howard's attitude and he has experienced the blessings of giving. Indeed, giving has been the most liberating area in Howard's Christian experience.

The Old and New Testaments place a great deal of emphasis on giving. In fact, there are more verses related to giving than any other subject on money. There are commands, practical suggestions, examples and exhortations concerning this facet of stewardship. Everywhere in the Bible covetousness and greed are condemned, and generosity and charity are encouraged.

ATTITUDE IN GIVING

Giving with the proper attitude is crucial. Read 1 Corinthians 13:3: "If I give away everything I own [to feed the poor] . . . but do not have love, I gain nothing." It is hard to imagine anything more commendable than giving everything to the poor. But if it is done with the wrong attitude, without love, it is of no benefit to the giver. The Lord set the example of giving motivated by love. "For God loved the world so much, that he gave his only Son" (John 3:16 GNT, emphasis added). Note the sequence: Because God loved, he gave.

We struggled for years to give consistently out of a heart of love. We believe the only way to do this is to recognize that each gift is actually given to the Lord himself. An example of this perspective is found in Numbers 18:24: "The tithe which the Israelites give as a contribution to the LORD" If giving is merely to a church, a ministry or to a needy person, it is only charity. But if it is to the Lord, it becomes an act of worship. Because Jesus Christ is our Creator, our Savior and our faithful Provider, we can express our gratefulness and love by giving our gifts to him. For example, when the offering plate is being passed

> *It is more blessed to give than to receive.*
>
> ACTS 20:35

at Mass, we should consciously remind ourselves that we are giving our gifts to the Lord himself.

Stop and examine yourself. What is your attitude toward giving? We cannot stress too much the importance of giving with the proper attitude.

ADVANTAGES OF GIVING

Of course, a gift benefits the recipient, but according to God's economy, if a gift is given with the proper attitude, the giver benefits more than the receiver. "Keep in mind the words of the Lord Jesus, that he himself said, 'It is more blessed to give than to receive'" (Acts 20:35). As we examine Scripture, we find the giver benefits in four significant areas.

1. Increase in Intimacy.

Above all else, giving directs our attention and hearts to Christ. Matthew 6:21 (GNT) tells us, "For your heart will always be where your riches are." This is why it is so necessary to go through the process of consciously giving each gift to the person of Jesus Christ. When you give your gift to him, your heart will automatically be drawn to the Lord.

2. Development of Character.

Our heavenly Father wants us as his children to be conformed to the image of his Son. The character of Christ is unselfish. Unfortunately, humans are by nature selfish. One of the key ways our character becomes conformed to Christ is by habitual giving. Someone once said, "Giving is not God's way of raising money; it is God's way of raising people into the likeness of his Son." The Lord understands that for us to develop into the people he wants us to be, we must learn how to share our possessions freely. If we don't, our inbred selfishness will grow and dominate us.

"An extreme example is Howard Hughes. In his youth Hughes was a typical playboy with a passion for parties and beautiful women and an aversion toward giving. As he grew older and turned an inheritance into a vast fortune, he became more and more closed-fisted. He let his wealth create an ever-increasing barrier between himself and other people. In his last years he lived in seclusion and became a recluse whose life was devoted to avoiding germs and people." [3]

Katherine Drexel is a sharp contrast to Hughes. Katherine also inherited wealth when her parents died while she was young. Rather than live from her inheritance, Katherine entered religious life and formed the Sisters of the Blessed Sacrament dedicated to the welfare of young Indian and black children. Over many years Katherine used her inheritance to build schools, hospitals and missions for the benefit of these children. St. Katherine displayed courage and initiative in addressing the social inequity among minorities—more than 100 years before they became issues of society. "Tell them to do good, . . . to be generous, ready to share . . . so as to win the life that is true life" (1 Timothy 6:18-19).

3. Investments for Eternity.

Matthew 6:20 (GNT) reads, "store up riches for yourselves in heaven, where moths and rust cannot destroy, and robbers cannot break in and steal." The Lord tells us that there really is something akin to the "First National Bank of Heaven." He wants us to know that we can invest for eternity.

Paul wrote, "It is not that I just want to receive gifts; rather, I want to see profit added to your account" (Philippians 4:17 GNT). So a permanent record really does exist for each of us in heaven! And we will be privileged to enjoy it forever. The Bible teaches that we "can't take it with us," but we can make deposits to our heavenly account before we die.

Randy Alcorn in his book *Money, Possessions and Eternity,* illustrates the wisdom and value of eternal investments.

Imagine for a moment that you are alive at the end of the Civil War. You are living in the South, but your home is really in the North. While in the South you have accumulated a good amount of Confederate currency. Suppose you know that the

72

North is going to win the war soon. What will you do with your Confederate money?

If you were smart there is only one answer to the question. You would cash in your Confederate currency for U.S. currency—the only money that will have value once the war is over. You would keep only enough Confederate currency to meet your basic needs for that short period until the war was over.

The currency of this world will be worthless at our death or at Christ's return, both of which are imminent. For us to accumulate vast earthly treasures in the face of the inevitable future is the equivalent to stockpiling Confederate money.[4]

The only currency of value in heaven is our present service and generous giving to God's kingdom. "Let us more and more insist on raising funds of love, of kindness, of understanding, of peace. Money will come if we seek first the Kingdom of God—the rest will be given" (Mother Teresa).

4. Increase in Blessings.

Many people have a hard time believing that giving results in blessings flowing to the giver. Proverbs 11:24-25 (GNT) reads, "Some people spend their money freely and still grow richer. Others are cautious, and yet grow poorer. Be generous."

Examine 2 Corinthians 9:6, 8: "Consider this: whoever sows sparingly will also reap sparingly, and whoever sows bountifully will also reap bountifully . . . Moreover, God is able to make every grace abundant for you, so that . . . you may have an abundance for every good work."

These verses clearly teach that giving results in blessings, but note carefully why the Lord returns blessings *Always having all you need, you may have an abundance for every good work . . . "* As shown on the diagram below, the Lord produces an increase so that we may give more and have our needs met at the same time.

THE AMOUNT TO GIVE

Let's survey what the Scriptures say about how much to give. Under the Old Testament a tithe, or 10 percent of a person's earnings, was required to be given. When the children of Israel disobeyed this commandment, it was regarded as robbing God himself. Listen to the Lord's solemn words in Malachi's days: "I ask you, is it right for a person to cheat God? Of course not, yet you are cheating me. 'How?' you ask. In the matter of tithes and offerings. A curse is on all of you because the whole nation is cheating me" (Malachi 3:8-9, GNT).

In addition to the tithe, the Hebrews were to give offerings. Furthermore, the Lord made special provisions for the needs of the poor. For example, every seven years all debts were forgiven, and special rules governed harvesting so that the poor could gather food.

In the New Testament the tithe is neither specifically rejected nor specifically recommended. It does teach us to give in proportion to the material blessing we have received, and it especially commends sacrificial giving.

What we like about the tithe or any fixed percentage of giving is that it is systematic, and the amount of the gift is easy to compute. The danger of the tithe is that it can be treated simply as another bill to be paid. By not giving out of a heart of love, we place ourself in a position where we can't receive the blessings the Lord has designed for a giver. Another potential danger of tithing is the view that once we have tithed, we've fulfilled all our obligations to give. For many the tithe should be the beginning of their giving, not the limit.

How much should you give?

To answer this question, first give yourself to the Lord. Submit yourself to him. Earnestly seek his will for you concerning giving. Ask him to help you obey Christ's leading. As disciples of Jesus, we have a responsibility to support the Church and contribute generously to the building up of the Body of Christ. Our emphasis shouldn't be on tithing, but on giving according to our means, using the tithe as our starting point. This can be a far more challenging norm, as it focuses not on how much we give away, but what we do with all of our resources.

The Abernathy family is an example. They used to own a shoe store. The members of the family had been praying that God would direct their sharing. As they prayed, they were impressed with the needs of the Wilsons, a large family in their community. Finances were tight for the Wilsons because the school year was starting. The Abernathys decided to give each of the five Wilson children two pairs of shoes. They didn't know that the shoes had been precisely what the Wilson children had been praying for.

Around the dinner table one evening the Wilson children again prayed for shoes. After they were finished with their prayers, their mother said, "You don't have to ask the Lord for shoes anymore. God has answered your prayers." One by one the shoes were brought out.

By the time it was over, the children thought God was in the shoe business! I wish you could have seen the sense of awe on the faces of the Abernathys as they experienced firsthand how God was directing their sharing through the quiet mystery of prayer.

How much do I have to give? We're sure that this thought has crossed your mind. The answer is that you don't have to give anything. As a good steward, you should be asking the question, "How much do I want to give?" The blessing that we have as good stewards is that we are free to give as much as we want. The whole question of giving shouldn't revolve around the "minimum" gift, but on the "maximum" gift. Our gifts should come from our heart and should be an indication of our faith (Cf. USCCB, *"Stewardship—A Disciple's Response; A Pastoral Letter on Stewardship,"*67).

THE PATTERN OF GIVING

During Paul's third missionary journey he wrote to the Corinthians concerning a promised collection to meet the needs of the persecuted believers in Jerusalem. "Every Sunday each of you must put aside some money, in proportion to what you have earned, and save it up, so that there will be no need to collect money when I come" (1 Corinthians 16:2, GNT). His comments provide practical instruction about giving. Let's call this pattern "Paul's Pod of P's," giving that is personal, periodic, private deposit and premeditated.

Giving should be personal

Giving is the privilege and responsibility of every Christian, young and old, rich and poor. "Each of you . . . " The benefits of giving are intended for each person to enjoy.

Several years ago Howard met a neighbor who loved to give. It was immediately apparent that he gained great pleasure from giving. Howard had never met a person like this before. As their relationship has grown, Howard has discovered how he learned to be a joyful giver. His parents shared generously with those in need and required each of their children to establish this habit. As a consequence, he continues to enjoy a level of freedom in sharing that few people experience.

Giving should be periodic

Periodic is the second of Paul's P's. The Lord understands that we need to give regularly, "every Sunday." Giving regularly helps draw us consistently to Christ.

Giving should be out of a private deposit

"Put aside some money . . . and save it up . . . ." If you experience difficulty in monitoring the money you have decided to give, consider opening a separate account. You might also do something as simple as setting aside a special "cookie jar" into which you deposit the money you intend to give.

The most gratifying part of setting aside money has been the thrill of praying that God would make us aware of needs and then enable us to respond.

Giving should be premeditated

Almost every Sunday Bev would ask Howard, "Honey, how much would you like to give this week at church?" His standard reply was, "I don't care. You make that decision." Because of Howard's cavalier attitude, he was not in a position to experience the blessing meant for the giver. To know the full joy and reap the blessing of giving, it must not be done carelessly. "You should each give, then, as you have decided, not with regret or out of a sense of duty; for God loves the one who gives gladly" (2 Corinthians 9:7, GNT). Our giving should involve thought, planning and prayer, exercising the same care in selecting where we give as we do when deciding where to invest. However, many believers operate like I used to—never thinking about giving until it is time for the collection.

The supreme example of premeditated giving was set by our Savior, "For the sake of the joy that lay before him he endured the cross" (Hebrews 12:2).

TO WHOM SHOULD WE GIVE?

We are told to share with three categories of people. To whom and in what proportion one gives varies with the needs God lays on the heart of each believer.

The Family

In our culture we are experiencing a tragic breakdown in this area of sharing. Husbands have failed to provide for their wives, parents have neglected their children, and grown sons and daughters have forsaken their elderly parents. Such neglect is solemnly condemned.

"And whoever does not provide for relatives and especially family members has denied the faith and is worse than an unbeliever" (1 Timothy 5:8). Meeting the needs of your family and relatives is the first priority in giving and one in which there should be no compromise.

The Local Church, Christian Workers and Ministries

Throughout its pages the Bible focuses on supporting the Lord's ministry. The Old Testament priesthood was to receive specific support (Numbers 18:21), and the New Testament teaching on ministry support is just as strong. "Presbyters who preside well deserve double honor, especially those who toil in preaching and teaching" (1 Timothy 5:17). How many Christian workers have been distracted from their ministry by inadequate support? Far too many.

People have asked Howard and Bev if they give only through their local church. In their case, the answer is no. However, giving a minimum of 10 percent of your income through your church is a tangible expression of your commitment to the church.

They also give to others who are directly having an influence on us. "One who is being instructed in the word should share all good things with his instructor" (Galatians 6:6).

The Poor

We didn't go to bed hungry last night, but conservative estimates are that one billion people in the world go to bed hungry each night. That is overwhelming. The number is so great that it may leave us feeling hopeless about what we can do. But Scripture consistently emphasizes our responsibility to give to the poor and the destitute.

In Matthew 25:34-45 we are confronted with one of the most exciting yet sobering truths in the Bible. Read this passage carefully:

Then the king will say . . ." For I was hungry and you gave me food, I was thirsty and you gave me drink . . . " Then the righteous will answer him and say, "Lord, when did we see you hungry and feed you, or thirsty and give you drink?" . . . And the king will say to them . . . "Amen, I say to you, whatever you did for one of these least brothers of mine, you did for me." Then he will say to those on his left, "Depart from me, you accursed, into the eternal fire . . . For I was hungry and you gave me no food, I was thirsty and you gave me no drink . . . what you did not do for one of these least ones, you did not do for me."

In some mysterious way that we cannot fully comprehend, Jesus personally identifies with the poor. Do you want to minister to Christ? You do so when you give to the poor. If that truth is staggering, then the reciprocal is terrifying. When we do not give to the poor, we leave Christ himself hungry and thirsty.

Three areas of Christian life are affected by our giving or our lack of giving to the poor.

1. Prayer.

A lack of giving to the poor could be the result of a hardened heart and a hardened heart is most often associated with a lack of prayer. "The kind of fasting I want is this: . . . share your bread with the hungry, and open your homes to the homeless . . . then my favor will shine on you . . . " (Isaiah 58:6-8 GNT). "Prayer does not seek superficial success, but rather the will of God and intimacy with him. God's apparent silence is itself an invitation to take a step farther — in total devotion, boundless faith, endless expectation. Anyone who prays must allow God the complete freedom to speak whenever he wants, to grant what ever he wants, and to give himself however he wants" (CCC2735-2737, *YOUCAT* 507).

2. Provision.

Our provision is conditioned upon our giving to the needy. "Give to the poor and you will never be in need. If you close your eyes to the poor, many people will curse you" (Proverbs 28:27 GNT).

3. Knowing Jesus Christ Intimately.

One who does not give to the poor does not know the Lord intimately. "Because he dispensed justice to the weak and the poor, he prospered. Is this not to know me?—oracle of the LORD" (Jeremiah 22:16).

Giving to the poor has been discouraged, in part, because of the government's failure with welfare programs. However, we challenge you to consider asking the Lord to bring one poor person into your life. This will be a significant step in your maturing in your relationship with Christ. We pray that you might be able to echo Job's statement: "For I rescued the poor who cried out for help, the orphans, and the unassisted . . . and the heart of the widow I made joyful . . . I was eyes to the blind, and feet to the lame was I; I was a father to the poor; the complaint of the stranger I pursued" (Job 29:12-16).

Although this area of giving can be frustrating at times, the potential benefits to the giver make it one of the most exciting and fulfilling areas in our entire Christian life.

CONTRAST

Society says: It is more blessed to receive than to give.

Scripture says: "It is more blessed to give than to receive" (Acts 20:35).

COMMITMENT

Establish a time each week when you can pray about giving.

TEN

WORK

Who Is Your Real Boss?

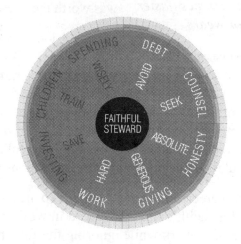

At age 29 Allen Hitchcock felt trapped. For six years he had worked as a clerk in a large department store.

He was competent, and the job paid moderately well. He longed, however, for a future in management, and as he looked around, he saw that all those who were promoted to management positions had college educations. So, by taking night courses, he completed his college requirements and earned a degree in business administration. The company soon promoted Allen to a job at a much higher salary.

The first few years were just as he had imagined—reasonable hours, good wages and attractive fringe benefits. Then the unexpected happened. The company expanded to Florida, and the Hitchcocks were transferred. The expansion schedule called for strict deadlines, and Allen assumed major responsibilities as an assistant manager. At first he enjoyed the excitement of the challenge; however, his five-day week soon became six, and his normal eight-hour day grew to 14 hours. On top of that, his new boss was so demanding that Allen began to experience a great deal of tension at work.

He now had more work and more responsibility, but as an assistant manager he no longer could earn overtime. As a result he made the same pay as he would have before the promotion, and resentment toward his employer was building. Allen began to wonder if management was worth the stress.

Sloth, like rust, consumes faster than labor wears.

–Benjamin Franklin

Allen's job frustrations are not unusual. Few people are completely satisfied with their jobs. Boredom, lack of fulfillment, fear of losing a job, inadequate wages, overwork and countless other pressures contribute to a high level of discontentment. Doctors, homemakers, secretaries, salespeople, blue-collar workers and managers—regardless of the profession, the frustrations are similar.

During a 50-year career the average person spends 100,000 hours working. Most of an adult's life is involved in work. Unfortunately, many just endure their work while ignoring the fact that 25 percent of their lives is devoted to a distasteful job. On the other hand, some people like work too much and neglect the other priorities of life.

People usually lean to one of two extremes: they either work as little as possible because work is unpleasant, or they tend to work all the time because it becomes overwhelmingly important. The Bible affirms the value of work but teaches that we should have a balance in work. Work is designed to develop our character. While enabling us to provide for our material well-being, work is a pathway to experiencing a closer relationship with the Lord and with other people. In order to find satisfaction and balance in our work, we need to understand what the Bible teaches about it.

BIBLICAL PERSPECTIVE OF WORK

The very first thing the Lord did with Adam was to assign him work. "Then the LORD God placed the man in the garden of Eden to cultivate it and guard it" (Genesis 2:15 GNT). "This human activity of cultivating and caring has a generic name: work. It is not a punishment for or a consequence of sin. True, sin does painfully skew the experience of work: 'By the sweat of your face shall you get bread to eat' (Gen 3:19). But, even so, God's mandate to humankind to collaborate with him in the task of creating—the command to work—comes before the Fall. Work is a fundamental aspect of the human vocation. It is necessary for human happiness and fulfillment. It is intrinsic to responsible stewardship of the world" (*Stewardship: A Disciple's Response*, USCCB, 25). After the Fall, work was made more difficult.

Work is so important that in Exodus 34:21 God gives this command: "For six days you shall labor, but on the seventh day you shall rest." The Old Testament believer was required to work six days. In the New Testament Paul is just as direct when he says, ". . . we instructed you that if anyone was unwilling to work, neither should that one eat" (2 Thessalonians 3:10). Examine the verse carefully. It says, "If anyone will not work." It did not say, "If anyone cannot work." This principle does not apply to those who are mentally or physically unable to work. It is for those who are able but choose not to work.

A primary purpose of work is to develop character. While the carpenter is building a house, the house is also building the carpenter. Skill, diligence, manual dexterity and judgment are refined. A job is not merely a task designed to earn money; it is also intended to produce godly character in the life of the worker.

A close friend has a sister who has been supported by her parents for more than 30 years. She has never had to face the responsibilities and hardships involved with a job. As a consequence, her character has not been properly developed and she is immature in many areas of her life.

HONORABLE PROFESSIONS

Scripture does not elevate any honest profession above another. There is dignity in all types of work, and a wide variety of vocations are represented in the Bible.

David was a shepherd and a king. Luke was a doctor. Lydia was a retailer who sold purple fabric. Daniel was a government worker. Paul was a tentmaker. Jesus, the Savior of the world, was a carpenter. In God's economy there is equal dignity in the labor of a salesperson and the president of a company, in the labor of a private and a general serving in the military.

A woman who works at a supermarket checkout counter writes: "I feel that my job consists of a lot more than ringing up orders, taking people's money, and bagging their groceries . . . By doing my job well I know I have a chance to do God's work too. Because of this, I try to make each of my customers feel special. While I'm serving them, they become the most important people in my life" (Maxine F. Dennis, in *Of Human Hands* [Minneapolis and Chicago; Augsburg Fortress/ACTA Publications, 1991], 49; *Stewardship: A Disciple's Response,* USCCB, 26-27).

GOD'S PART IN WORK

The Bible reveals three specific responsibilities the Lord has in connection with work.

1. God gives job skills.

Exodus 36:1 (GNT) illustrates this truth: "Bezalel, Oholiab, and all the other workers to whom the LORD has given skill and understanding, who know how to make everything needed to build the sacred Tent are to make everything just as the LORD has commanded." God has given each of us unique skills. People have widely varied abilities, manual skills and intellectual capacities. It is not a matter of one person being better than another; it is simply a matter of having received different capabilities.

2. God gives success.

The life of Joseph is a perfect example. "The LORD was with Joseph and made him successful. He lived in the house of his Egyptian master, who saw that the LORD was with Joseph and had made him successful in everything he did" (Genesis 39:2-3 GNT). As we have seen, you and I have certain responsibilities, but we need to recognize that it is ultimately God who gives success.

3. God, in his sovereignty, controls promotion.

Psalm 75:7-8 reads, "For judgment comes not from east or from west, not from the desert or from the mountains, but from God who decides, who brings some low and raises other high." As much as it may surprise you, your boss is not the one who controls whether or not you will be promoted. When you understand this, you will work with a different attitude. It should have a tremendous impact on the way you perform as an employee.

This perspective of God's part in work is a remarkable contrast to the way most people think. Most leave God out of work and believe that they alone control their success and promotions. However, those with a biblical understanding will approach work with an entirely different frame of reference. They can avoid one of the major reasons people experience stress and frustration in their jobs because they understand God's part in work.

Stop reading for a few minutes and think about that. God gives you your skills and through his sovereignty and you, through your own free, will control your success and promotion. Think about how this change in perspective will influence you and your job.

OUR PART IN WORK

All of us have certain responsibilities related to our work. Scripture reveals we are actually serving the Lord in our work and not people. "Whatever you do, work at it with all your heart, as though you were working for the Lord and not for people. Remember that the Lord will give you as a reward what he has kept for his people.

For Christ is the real Master you serve" (Colossians 3:23-24 GNT). This perspective has profound implications. Consider your attitude toward work. If you could see the person of Jesus Christ as your boss, would you try to be more faithful in your job? The most important question you need to answer every day as you begin your work is: For whom do I work? You work for Christ.

Work hard.

"Work hard at whatever you do . . . " (Ecclesiastes 9:10 GNT). "The diligent man will get precious wealth." (Proverbs 12:27 RSVCE). In the Bible hard work and diligence are encouraged while laziness is repeatedly condemned: "A lazy person is as bad as someone who is destructive" (Proverbs 18:9 GNT).

Paul's life was an example of hard work. " . . . Instead, we worked and toiled; we kept working day and night so as not to be an expense to any of you. We did this, not because we do not have the right to demand our support; we did it to be an example for you to follow" (2 Thessalonians 3:8-9 GNT). Your work should be at such a level that people will never equate laziness and mediocrity with God.

But do not overwork! Working too hard has reached epidemic proportions. A frantic, breathless over commitment to work pervades our culture. Hard work must be balanced with the other priorities of life. Clearly our first priority is our relationship with the Lord. "But seek first the kingdom [of God] and His righteousness" (Matthew 6:33). The second priority is the family.

If your job demands so much of your time and energy that you neglect your relationship with Christ or your family, then you are working too hard; perhaps the job is too demanding or your work habits need changing. If you tend to be a "workaholic," take extra precautions to guard against forsaking your other priorities.

Exodus 34:21 (GNT) reads, "You have six days in which to do your work, but do not work on the seventh day, not even during plowing time or harvest." This Old Testament principle of resting one day out of seven has application for us today. This has been difficult for us, particularly when we are working under the pressure of a project deadline or financial pressure.

Rest can become an issue of faith. Is the Lord able to make our six days of work more productive than seven days? Yes! The Lord instituted this weekly rest for our physical, mental and spiritual health. The diagram below illustrates the balance God wants in our lives.

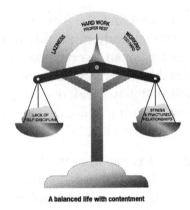

A balanced life with contentment

EMPLOYER'S RESPONSIBILITIES

The godly employer must perform a balancing act. The employer is to love, serve and encourage the employee, but he or she must also provide leadership and hold employees accountable for their assigned tasks. Let's examine several principles that should govern an employer's conduct.

Serve your employees

The basis for biblical leadership is servanthood: " . . . If one of you wants to be great, you must be the servant of the rest . . . " (Matthew 20:26 GNT). Too often employers have concentrated on producing a profit at the expense of their personnel. However, the Bible directs the employer to balance profit-making efforts with an unselfish concern for the employees. Employees are to be treated fairly and with genuine dignity. "Masters [employers], be fair and just in the way you treat your slaves [employees]. Remember that you too have a Master in heaven" (Colossians 4:1 GNT).

Employers should seek creative ways to serve their subordinates. For example, they should consider investing time and money to educate and upgrade their employees' job skills. As employees become more capable, both employees and companies can earn more.

Be a good communicator

The biblical account of building the Tower of Babel teaches the importance of good communication. At that time everyone spoke the same language and adopted a common goal of building the tower. The Lord makes this remarkable observation: ". . . Now then, these are all one people and they speak one language; this is just the beginning of what they are going to do. Soon they will be able to do anything they want!" (Genesis 11:6, GNT)

Since building the tower was not what the Lord wanted, he stopped construction. And how did the Lord do this? He disrupted their ability to communicate. "Let us go down and mix up their language so they will not understand each other" (Genesis 11:7, GNT).

It is especially important to listen to employee complaints. "When any of my servants complained against me, I would listen and treat them fairly. If I did not, how could I then face God? What could I say when God came to judge me?" (Job 31:13-14 GNT). A sensitive, listening ear is a tangible expression that you care about the other person. When a complaint is legitimate, the employer should take appropriate steps to solve the problem.

Hold employees accountable

The employer is responsible for letting employees know what is expected of them on the job. The employer should regularly evaluate their performances and communicate this to them. If an employee is not performing satisfactorily and is unable or unwilling to change, a personnel change may be necessary.

Pay your employees a fair wage promptly

Employers are warned to pay a fair wage. "[The Lord will judge] those who defraud the hired man of his wages" (Malachi 3:5). They are also commanded to pay wages promptly when due. "Do not cheat poor and needy hired servants…Each day before sunset pay them for that day's work…If you do not pay them, they will cry out against you to the LORD and you will be guilty of sin" (Deuteronomy 24:14-15 GNT). Tobit reiterates this message, "Pay your workers each day; never keep back their wages overnight. Honor God in this way, and he will reward you" (Tobit 4:14 GNT).

EMPLOYEE'S RESPONSIBILITIES

We can identify the six major responsibilities of the godly employee by examining the well-known story of Daniel in the lions' den. In Daniel chapter 6 we are told that Darius, the king of Babylon, appointed 120 men to administer the government and three men, one of whom was Daniel, to supervise these administrators. When King Darius decided to promote Daniel to the job of governing the entire kingdom, Daniel's fellow employees tried to eliminate him. They first looked for an opportunity to discredit him in his job. After this failed, they persuaded King Darius to make a foolish decree. For a period of 30 days everyone in the kingdom would be required to worship the king only or suffer the punishment of death in the lions' den. Daniel was thrown to the lions because he continued to worship the living God. The Lord then rescued this godly employee by sending His angel to shut the lions' mouths.

Diligence is the mother

of good fortune.

—Cervantes

Let's examine the attributes of a godly employee as modeled by Daniel.

Honest

Daniel 6:5 tells us that Daniel's fellow employees could find no grounds for accusation against him in regard to his work. "No fault or corruption" could be found in Daniel's work. He was absolutely honest. We studied the importance of honesty earlier in the book.

Faithful

In Daniel 6:5, Daniel is described as "trustworthy." The godly employee needs to establish the goal of being faithful and excellent in work. Then he or she needs to work hard to attain that goal.

Prayerful

The godly employee is a person of prayer. "When Daniel learned that the order had been signed [restricting worship to the king alone] . . . just as he had always done, he knelt down at the open windows and prayed to God three times a day" (Daniel 6:10 GNT).

Daniel governed the most powerful nation of his day. Few of us will ever be faced with the magnitude of his responsibilities and the time demands that must have been required. Yet this man knew the importance and priority of prayer. If you are not praying consistently, your work is suffering.

Honor Your Employer

"Daniel answered, 'May your Majesty live forever!'" (Daniel 6:21 GNT). What a remarkable response! The king, his employer, had been deceived and was forced into sentencing Daniel to the lions' den. But Daniel's reaction was to honor his boss. Think how natural it would have been to say something like, "You dummy! The God who sent his angel to shut the lions' mouths is going to punish you!" Instead, he honored his employer.

The godly employee always honors his superior. In 1 Peter 2:18 (GNT) we read, "You servants [employees], must submit yourselves to your masters [employers] and show them complete respect, not only to those who are kind and considerate, but also to those who are harsh." One way to honor your employer is never to participate in gossip behind your employer's back—even if he or she is not an ideal person.

Honor Fellow Employees

People will play "office politics" and may attempt to secure a promotion over you. They might even have you terminated from your job. Daniel's peers tried to murder him. Despite this, no evidence exists that Daniel did anything but honor his fellow employees. Never slander a fellow employee. "Never criticize servants [employee] to their master [employer]. You will be cursed and will suffer for it" (Proverbs 30:10, GNT).

The godly person should avoid office politics and manipulation to secure a promotion. Your superior does not control your promotion. The Lord himself through his sovereignty and you, through your free, will make that determination. We can be content in our jobs by striving for faithfulness, honoring superiors, loving and encouraging our fellow employees. Christ will promote us if and when he chooses.

Verbalize Your Faith

At the appropriate time Daniel spoke of his faith in God to those around him. "He [the King] called out anxiously, 'Daniel, servant of the living God! Was the God you serve so loyally able to save you from the lions?'" (Daniel 6:20 GNT).

King Darius would never have known about the living God if Daniel had not communicated his faith at appropriate moments during the normal conduct of his job. King Darius would not have been as powerfully influenced by Daniel's profession of faith in God if he had not observed how he did his work. Daniel fulfilled his responsibilities with honesty and faithfulness while honoring those around him. Because of this demonstration, coupled with Daniel's deliverance from the lions, Darius became a believer: "I decree that throughout my royal domain the God of Daniel is to be reverenced and feared: for he is the living God enduring forever; his kingdom shall not be destroyed and his dominion shall be without end" (Daniel 6:27).

Daniel influenced his employer, one of the most powerful people in the world, to believe in the only true God. You have that same opportunity in your own God-given sphere of work. Let us say this another way. A job well done earns you the right to tell others with whom you work about the reality of Christ. As we view our work from God's perspective, dissatisfaction will turn to contentment from a job well done, and drudgery will be replaced with excitement over the prospect of introducing others to the Savior.

RETIREMENT

The dictionary defines retirement as "withdrawal from an occupation or business, to give up or retreat from an active life." The goal of retirement is deeply ingrained in our culture. Many people retire at an arbitrary, predetermined age and cease all labor in the pursuit of a life filled with leisure.

The Bible gives no examples of people retiring. Only one direct reference to retirement is found in the Bible. It is in Numbers 8:24-26; the instruction there applied exclusively to the Levites who worked on the tabernacle. As long as one is physically and mentally capable, no scriptural basis exists for retiring and becoming unproductive. The concept of putting an older but able person "out to pasture" is unbiblical. Age is no obstacle to finishing the work the Lord has for you to accomplish. For example, Moses was 80 years old when he began his 40-year task of leading the children of Israel.

Scripture does indicate that the type and intensity of work may change as we grow older—shifting gears to a less demanding pace and to becoming an "elder at the gate." During this season of life we can actively employ the experience and wisdom gained over a lifetime. I believe this should be the most rewarding and productive time of life. God has invested years in grooming us, and often we have more discretionary time.

Forget retirement. Grasp the opportunity to help build God's kingdom!

CALLING

Every Christian has a specific calling or purpose which the Lord intends for us to fulfill in our work. The Second Vatican Council points out that, "through work, we build up not only our world but the Kingdom of God, already present among us. Work is a partnership with God—our share in a divine human collaboration in creation. It occupies a central place in our lives as Christian Stewards" (*Stewardship: A Disciple's Response,* USCCB, Appendix 1,43).

Ephesians 2:10 (GNT) reads, "God has made us what we are, and in our union with Christ Jesus he has created us for a life of good deeds, which he has already prepared for us to do." Study this passage carefully. "God has made us what we are." Each of us has been created uniquely and given special physical, emotional and mental characteristics and abilities. You probably have heard the expression, "After the Lord made you, he threw away the mold!" It's true. You are gifted uniquely. No one in all of history—past, present or future—is like you.

The passage continues, "and in our union with Christ Jesus he has created us for a life of good deeds, which he has already prepared for us to do." The Lord created each of us for a particular job, and he endowed us with the necessary skills, aptitudes and desires to accomplish this work. This calling may be fulltime Christian service or a secular job. Often people struggle to know whether God wants them to continue in business once they have committed their lives to Christ. Many feel they are not serving the Lord in a significant way if they remain in a secular job. Nothing could be further from the truth. The key is for each person to determine God's call on his or her life.

Past experiences prepare us for our calling

God providentially allows us to experience circumstances to prepare us for our calling. You might find it difficult to believe that God was molding you through your family, your education, your work and your relationships, especially if these were not godly influences. Nonetheless, he was preparing you even in the difficult experiences. For example, the Lord might use a painful, unwanted situation to give someone the empathy and desire to serve others in a similar situation.

Knowing our calling allows us to focus

Most of us struggle with too many things to do and too little time in which to do them. The good can become the enemy of the best. Once you have a clear vision of God's call on your life, it becomes much easier to evaluate opportunities and say "no" to those that would distract you from what the Lord wants you to accomplish.

Howard has two close friends. One has only average ability, but because he has been singled-minded in his focus he has had an enormous impact. The other man is much more capable but has scattered his energies pursuing numerous projects with limited success. Knowing your calling helps you focus and become more productive.

CONTRAST

Society says: Work as little as possible because labor is distasteful; or work as much as possible because your job is all-important.

Scripture says: Work as unto the Lord with faithfulness as your standard. Work hard, but do not overwork.

COMMITMENT

Prayerfully evaluate your attitudes toward work and your job performance in light of what the Bible teaches. To help you discover any areas that need changing, ask yourself these questions:

1. Would I work more conscientiously if Jesus were my boss?

2. Would I think more highly of a president of an oil company than a gas station attendant?

3. How is my relationship with my employer, or employees and fellow workers?

4. Am I trying to do too much?

5. Am I performing my job at a level of excellence?

6. Am I lazy? Do I work hard?

ELEVEN

INVESTING

Steady Plodding

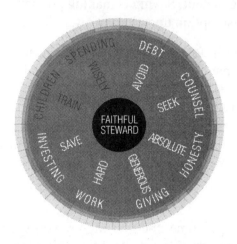

One problem Allen and Jean wanted to discuss was their inability to save. "We've never been able to save consistently," Jean admitted dejectedly. "We realize this has been a mistake, and we've suffered for it. Every time the car broke down or something else went wrong, we ended up going further in debt because we didn't have savings to pay for these unexpected expenses. What should we do?"

Allen added, "And how can we begin to invest to help provide for future needs such as our children's education and our retirement?"

Unfortunately, like the Hitchcocks, most people are not regular savers. According to one source, the average person in our nation is three weeks away from bankruptcy. They have little or no money saved, and completely depend on the next paycheck to make ends meet.

SAVING—THE JOSEPH PRINCIPLE

The Bible tells us it's wise to save. "Precious treasure remains in the house of the wise, but the fool consumes it" (Proverbs 21:20).

Because of their instinct for saving, ants are commended for their wisdom: "Four things are among the smallest on the earth, and yet are exceedingly wise: Ants—a species not strong yet they store up their food in the summer" (Proverbs 30:24-25). They put aside and save from the summer's plenty to meet a future need. Saving is the opposite of being in debt. Saving is making provision for tomorrow, while debt is presumption upon tomorrow.

Another example is Joseph, who saved during the seven years of plenty to ensure that there would be enough food during seven years of famine. I call saving the "Joseph Principle." Saving means to forgo an expenditure today so you will have something to spend in the future. Perhaps this is why most people never save; it requires a denial of something that you want today, and our culture isn't a culture of denial. When we want something, we want it now.

HOW TO SAVE

When you receive income, the first money you spend should be a gift to the Lord, and the second should go to savings. An automatic payroll deduction is a great way to save. Some people save their tax refunds or bonuses. Remember this: if you immediately save, you'll save more.

The Bible doesn't teach an amount to be saved. We recommend saving ten percent of your income. This may not be possible initially. But begin the habit of saving—even if it's only a dollar a month.

Long-Term Savings

Long-term savings are intended to fund long-term needs and goals such as retirement income and inheritances. Pensions and retirement accounts fall into this category. Except for extreme financial emergencies, these savings should not be used for any other purpose.

Short-Term Savings

Short-term savings should be readily accessible. They may include interest-bearing accounts, mutual funds and so forth. These are designed to be used for planned future spending—acquiring or replacing items such as appliances and cars and making major home repairs. Short-term savings should also be set aside for emergencies— an illness, loss of job, or other interruption of income. Financial experts recommend you establish the goal of saving the equivalent of three to six months of your income for this emergency fund.

INVESTING

People place some of their savings in investments with the expectation of receiving income or a growth in value. The purpose and intention of this book is not to recommend any specific investments. Our objective is simply to draw your attention to the following scriptural framework for investing.

Be a Steady Plodder

"The plans of the diligent are sure of profit but all rash haste leads certainly to poverty" (Proverbs 21:5). The original Hebrew word for "steady plodding" pictures a person filling a large barrel, one handful at a time. Little by little the barrel is filled to overflowing.

The fundamental principle you need to practice to become a successful investor is to spend less than you earn. Then save and invest the difference over a long period of time.

Examine various investments. Almost all of them are well suited to "steady plodding." Your home mortgage is paid off after years of steady payments. A stock portfolio is built as it is added to each month, and a business can increase steadily in value through the years as its potential is developed.

Understand Compound Interest

Albert Einstein once said, "Compounding is the greatest mathematical discovery of all time, not E=mc2." Compounding occurs when the earnings your investments produce are added to the principle, allowing both the earnings and the principle to grow exponentially. There are three variables in compounding: the amount you save, the interest rate you earn on your savings and the length of time you save.

1. The amount.

The amount you save depends upon your income and spending. It's our hope that you will be able to increase the amount available for saving as you learn God's way of handling money.

2. The rate.

The second variable is the rate you earn on an investment. The following table demonstrates how an investment of $1,000 a year grows at various rates.

Rate Earned	Year 5	Year 10	Year 20	Year 30	Year 40
6%	$5,975	$13,972	$38,993	$83,802	$164,048
8%	$6,336	$15,645	$49,423	$122,346	$279,781
10%	$6,716	$17,531	$63,003	$180,943	$486,851
12%	$7,115	$19,655	$80,699	$270,293	$859,142

As you can see, the increase in the rate of return has a remarkable impact on the amount accumulated. A two percent increase almost doubles the amount over 40 years. But since higher returns usually also carry higher risks, be careful not to shoot for unrealistic returns.

3. The time.

Time is the third factor. The following graph will help you visualize the benefits of compounding. If a person saves $2.74 a day—$1,000

98

a year—and earns 10 percent, at the end of forty years the savings will grow to $526,985 and will be earning $4,392 each month. However, if the person waits one year before starting, then saves for 39 years, the result won't be just $1,000 less; it will be $50,899 less! Compounding is your friend, and the earlier you can start it working for you, the better. Start saving and investing today!

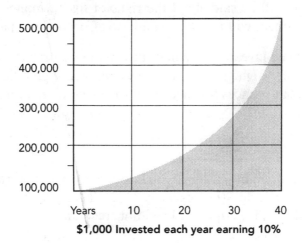

$1,000 Invested each year earning 10%

Avoid Risky Investments

"Here is a terrible thing that I [Solomon] have seen in this world: people save up their money for a time when they may need it and then lose it all in some bad deal and end up with nothing left to pass on to their children. We leave this world just as we entered it—with nothing. In spite of all our work there is nothing we can take with us" (Ecclesiastes 5:13-15, GNT).

The Bible warns of avoiding risky investments, yet each year thousands of people lose money in highly speculative and sometimes fraudulent investments. How many times have you heard of older people losing their life's savings on a get-rich-quick scheme? Sadly, it seems that Christians are particularly vulnerable to such schemes because they trust people who seem to live by the same values they have. There are three characteristics often associated with risky investments:

- The prospect of a large profit is "practically guaranteed."

- The decision to invest must be made quickly. There will be no opportunity to thoroughly investigate the investment or the promoter who is selling the investment. The promoter will often be doing you a "favor" by allowing you to invest.

- Little will be said about the risks of losing money, and the investment will usually require no effort on your part.

Be patient when investing. We have never known anyone who made money in a hurry. Diligence, study and counsel are prerequisites for improving your chances for successful investments and for avoiding risky ones.

Diversify

"Make seven or eight portions; you know not what misfortune may come upon the earth" (Ecclesiastes 11:2). There is no investment without risk, and Scripture does not recommend any specific investments. Money can be lost on any investment. The government can make gold illegal. Real estate can suffer deflation or be taxed from you. Money can be inflated until it is valueless.

The perfect investment doesn't exist. We need to diversify. Consider the following steps as you diversify. Don't skip any of the steps. Start with step one, and take each step at a time.

Step 1: Save one month's living expenses and secure insurance protection.

Step 2: Save three to six months' living expenses; save for major purchases; develop your business and vocational skills.

A principle in Scripture is to invest in your business or vocation, which will be productive, then build your house: "Complete your outdoor tasks, and arrange your work in the field; afterward you can build your house" (Proverbs 24:27). Many people today reverse this order. The large house, purchased too early in life, tends to require so much money that investing in business or vocation is seriously hampered.

Step 3: Purchase a home; invest conservatively to meet long-term goals.

Step 4: Make other investments.

George Fooshee talks about such investments in his excellent book, You Can Be Financially Free.[5]

> Other investments are almost as varied as the imagination. Real estate, oil, stocks, bonds, antiques, coins, and virtually anything people collect can be considered investments. Some of these, such as stocks, bonds, and real estate, pay a return. Others are held with the expectation that they will increase in value at time goes by.

> Your investments beyond life insurance, vocation, and house should be matched with your own interests and personality. If you were raised on a farm and have knowledge of agricultural products and enjoy keeping abreast of the farm situation, then you might pursue a lifelong interest in agricultural investments. These could include everything from acquiring farmland to purchasing the stocks of those companies that are primarily agriculturally oriented.

Count the Cost

With every investment there are costs: financial costs, time commitments and efforts required. Sometimes investments can bring emotional stress. For example, the purchase of a rental house will require time and effort to lease and maintain. If the tenant is irresponsible, you may have to try to collect rent from someone who does not want to pay. Talk about emotions flaring! Before you decide on any investment, carefully consider all the costs.

Now we will shift our attention to a number of issues that are important to understand from God's perspective: balancing saving with giving, investment goals, gambling and leaving an inheritance.

GIVING, SAVING AND INVESTING

It is scripturally permissible to save and invest only when we are also giving. Jesus told a parable that illustrates the danger of saving while not giving.

> There was a rich man whose land produced a bountiful harvest. He asked himself, 'What shall I do, for I do not have space to store my harvest?' And he said, 'This is what I shall do: I shall tear down my barns and build larger ones. There I shall store all my grain and other goods and I shall say to myself, "Now as for you, you have so many good things stored up for many years, rest, eat, drink, be merry!"' But God said to him, 'You fool, this night your life will be demanded of you; and the things you have prepared, to whom will they belong?' Thus will it be for the one who stores up treasure for himself but is not rich in what matters to God...For where your treasure is, there also will your heart be (Luke 12:16-21, 34).

Precious treasure remains in the house of the wise, but the fool consumes it.

Proverbs 21:20

The key word in this parable is "**all**." Jesus called the rich man a fool because he saved all of his goods, laying them up for his own use. He did not balance his saving by giving generously. It is legitimate to save and invest only when we are also giving to the Lord. Why? "For where your treasure is, there also will your heart be" (Matthew 6:21).

If we concentrate solely on saving and investing, our focus and affection will gravitate there. We will be drawn inexorably to those possessions. But if we balance our saving and investing by giving generously to the Lord, we can still love Christ first with all our heart.

INVESTMENT GOALS

Before you develop your individual investment strategy, you should establish investment goals. We believe there are four acceptable goals for investing.

1. Providing for Your Family.

See 1 Timothy 5:8: "And whoever does not provide for relatives and especially family members has denied the faith and is worse than an unbeliever." This principle extends to providing for your needs in old age and leaving an inheritance to your children.

2. Becoming Financially Free to Serve the Lord.

One objective of saving is to diminish our dependence upon a salary to meet our needs. This affords us the freedom to volunteer more time to ministry should this be what the Lord wants for us. The more my savings produce, the less I'm dependent upon income from my work. Some have saved enough to be free one day a week, and others are in a position to be full-time volunteers without the need to earn a salary.

3. Operating Your Business.

It is proper to save and invest to accumulate enough capital to operate a business without going into debt. The amount of capital may vary substantially, depending upon the requirements of each business.

4. Establishing a Maximum Amount.

When a sprinter breaks the tape at the finish line, he stops running. But many people continue accumulating more and more, even though they have achieved acceptable savings goals. Each of us should establish a maximum amount we are going to accumulate, and once we have "finished the race," we should give away the portion of our income that we were saving. This "finish line" on accumulation protects us against the dangers of hoarding.

UNACCEPTABLE INVESTMENT GOALS

According to 1 Timothy 6:9-11 one investment goal, the desire to become rich, is strictly prohibited; 1 Timothy 6:9 states, "Those who want to be rich are falling into temptation and into a trap and into many foolish and harmful desires, which plunge them into ruin and destruction." Study this carefully. Everyone who wants to get rich will "fall into temptation and into a trap and into many foolish and harmful desires, which plunge men into ruin and destruction."

For most of Howard's life he wanted to become rich—not just a little rich; filthy rich! So dealing with the biblical prohibition against this attitude has been painful for him. Sometimes even now he vacillates between wanting to get rich and wanting to be a faithful steward. When he wants to get rich, he is self-centered. His motivations for wanting to get rich may vary—pride, greed or an unhealthy compulsion to prepare for survival in an uncertain economic future. However, when he focuses on being a faithful steward, he is Christ-centered in his thoughts and attitudes. Howard's actions are then motivated by a pure heart. He is serving Christ and growing closer to him.

The prohibition against wanting to get rich in 1 Timothy 6:9 is followed by this passage: "For the love of money is the root of all evils..." (1 Timothy 6:10). In other words, when we want to get rich, Scripture tells us that we are loving money.

Matthew 6:24 says: "No one can serve two masters. He will either hate one and love the other, or be devoted to one and despise the other. You cannot serve God and mammon.[money]." Think about this carefully. When we want to get rich, we are actually loving money and hating God. We are holding on to money and despising God. We are serving money, and we are therefore not serving the living God. First Timothy 6:10 ends by saying, "some people in their desire for it have strayed from the faith and have pierced themselves with many pains."

Sin causes people to turn in on themselves; to become grasping and exploitative toward possessions and other people; to grow accustomed to conducting relationships not by the standards of generous stewardship, but by the calculus of self-interest: 'What's in it for me?' Constantly, Christians must beg God for the grace of conversion: the grace to know who they are, to whom they belong, how they are to live—the grace to repent and change and grow, the grace to become good disciples and stewards (*Stewardship: A Disciple's Response,* USCCB, 28).

Howard has witnessed firsthand the truth of this scripture. He deeply admired the man who led him to Christ, but he became consumed by a desire to get rich. He divorced his wife and abandoned his four young sons. Ultimately, he denied Christ and wandered away from the faith. Wanting to get rich, which is the love of money, is a devastating spiritual condition in which to be.

Understand us clearly. We are not saying getting rich is wrong. In fact, we rejoice to see God sovereignly enable a man or woman to prosper. Nothing is wrong with becoming wealthy if it is a by-product of being a faithful steward.

SPLIT AND SUBMIT

We overcome the temptation to get rich by remembering to split and submit. When you become aware of your desire to become rich, you must flee (split) from that temptation and replace it with the pursuit of godliness.

Next, submit. The ultimate way of escape is found in submitting to Jesus as Lord. We can do this in perfect confidence because Jesus overcame a massive temptation to become rich. After Christ fasted 40 days in the wilderness, the devil tempted him three times. The final temptation is recorded in Luke 4:5-7: "Then he [the devil] took him up and showed him all the kingdoms of the world in a single instant. The devil said to him, 'I shall give to you all this power and their glory . . . if you worship me.'" Can you imagine what an incredible temptation this would present?

When Howard was in the real estate development business and discovered a prime piece of property, he would almost immediately begin to covet it and revel in the possibility of becoming rich. Jesus was exposed to all the kingdoms of the world in a moment of time. But because he was submitted entirely to the Father and empowered by the same Holy Spirit who lives in us, he was able to resist that temptation.

Our heavenly Father will never ultimately prosper his children when they are motivated to get rich. Wanting to get rich—loving money— closely parallels greed. And "greed . . . amounts to idolatry" (Colossians 3:5). The Father watches jealously over his children to ensure that we will not be drawn away from loving him with all our hearts.

GAMBLING AND LOTTERIES

Government-sanctioned lotteries and all types of gambling are sweeping our nation. A recent study reported that the average church member gives $20 a year to foreign missions while the average person gambles $400 a year! Sadly, there are hundreds of thousands of compulsive gamblers who regularly deplete their family income. Their stories are heartbreaking. The Bible does not specifically prohibit gambling; however, many who gamble do so in an attempt to get rich quickly. This is a violation of Scripture.

As men and women who serve a holy God, we are called to be salt and light to a lost world. We should make a commitment to never participate in gambling or lotteries even for entertainment. We should not expose ourselves to the risk of becoming compulsive gamblers, nor should we support an industry that enslaves so many.

INHERITANCE

Parents should attempt to leave a material inheritance to their children. "Good people will have wealth to leave to their grandchildren" (Proverbs 13:22 GNT). The inheritance should not be dispensed until the child has been thoroughly trained to be a wise steward. "The more easily you get your wealth, the less good it will do you" (Proverbs 20:21 GNT).

An inheritance should be distributed over several years or when the heir is mature enough to handle the responsibility of money. Select those you trust to supervise the youth until he or she is a capable steward. "The son who will receive his father's property is treated just like a slave while he is young, even though he really owns everything.

While he is young, there are men who take care of him and manage his affairs until the time set by his father" (Galatians 4:1-2 GNT).

You should provide an inheritance for your children. However, it probably is not wise to leave your children with great wealth if they have not been thoroughly schooled in the biblical perspective of money and how to properly manage it. Andrew Carnegie once said, "The almighty dollar bequeathed to a child is an almighty curse. No one has the right to handicap his children with such a burden as great wealth. He must face this question squarely: Will the fortune be safe with my child, and will my child be safe with my fortune?"

WILLS

The majority of people who die do not have a current will. Think of what this means in the United States. To die without a will is expensive and time-consuming and can be heartbreaking for your loved ones. It can literally destroy an estate left to provide for the family.

The Bible teaches that we brought nothing into the world and we will take nothing with us when we die, but we can leave it behind precisely as we wish. We can specify to whom and how much. If you die without a will, these decisions are left up to the court. Under some circumstances the court can appoint a guardian (who may not know the Lord) to raise your children if you have not made this provision in your will.

Whether you are married or single, rich or poor, you should have a will. Not only does it clear up any legal uncertainties, it also helps you map out your finances while you are alive so that you can protect the best interests of your heirs.

About 36 out of 100 people die before retirement age. So do not put off preparation of your will just because you may be young. Do it now! As Isaiah told Hezekiah, ". . . The LORD tells you that you are to put everything in order, because you will not recover. Get ready to die" (2 Kings 20:1 GNT). Someday, you will die. One of the greatest gifts you can leave your family for that emotional time will be an organized estate and a properly prepared will or revocable living trust. If you don't have a current will or trust, please make an appointment with an attorney to prepare one.

CONTRAST

Society says: Spend all you make. However, if you should save, put your trust in your accumulated assets.

Scripture says: "Precious treasure remains in the house of the wise, but the fool consumes it" (Proverbs 21:20).

COMMITMENT

1. Establish a pattern of saving. Start with your next paycheck.

2. Make an appointment with an attorney this week to have your will drawn.

TWELVE

THE ONE GUARANTEED INVESTMENT

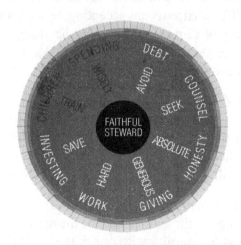

Howard was 28 years old when he stumbled upon the only fully guaranteed investment that exists. He started attending a weekly breakfast with several young businessmen and was impressed because they were astute and energetic. But more than that, he was attracted to the quality of their lives.

At the time Howard was part owner of a successful restaurant. He was married to his wonderful wife, Bev, and lived in a comfortable home. He had everything he thought would give him happiness and a sense of accomplishment, but he felt neither. Something was missing. Howard was surprised to hear these men speak openly of their faith in God. He had attended church regularly as he was growing up. However, he never heard that it was possible to have a personal relationship with Jesus Christ.

Through the attendance at Mass and reception of the sacraments, have we really developed a personal relationship with Jesus Christ? Knowing Christ and going to church are not the same thing. In his book *Rediscovering Catholicism* Matthew Kelly writes "As modern day Catholics, many of us seem content to attend Mass on Sunday and send our children to Catholic schools and worship the gods of materialism and secularism the other 167 hours of the week."

Part of the mission of the Church is to help us progress from knowing about Jesus as a historical person and teacher, to personally knowing the risen Lord as Savior. "Conversion means accepting, by a personal decision, the saving sovereignty of Christ and becoming his disciple" (John Paul II, *Redemptoris Missio (Mission of the Redeemer)* Washington, DC: United States Conference of Catholic Bishops, 1991, 46).

Part of being a disciple is recognizing that we are all sinners and that our sins can separate us from God. "All have sinned and are deprived of the glory of God" (Romans 3:23) and that because of our sins Christ died on the cross; "God proves his love for us in that while we were still sinners Christ died for us" (Romans 5:8).

In John 14:6 we learned that Jesus is "the way and the truth and the life. No one comes to the Father except through me." Life on earth is our preparation for eternity with our Father, and if the only way to go to our Father is through Jesus—a close personal relationship with Jesus Christ is paramount.

In order to build and grow our relationship with Jesus, we must realize that God loves us immensely; "For God so loved the world that he gave his only Son, so that everyone who believes in him might not perish but might have eternal life. For God did not send his Son into the world to condemn the world, but that the world might be saved through him" (John 3:16-17).

Our salvation is God's gift to us; how we live our life is our gift to God. "For by grace you have been saved through faith, and this is not from you; it is the gift of God; it is not from works, so no one may boast." (Ephesians 2:8-9). "Conversion to Christ involves making a genuine commitment to him and a personal decision to follow him as his disciple" (*National Directory for Catechesis*, 48).

Jesus Christ's plan for our lives is so much better than anything we could imagine for ourselves because of his amazing love for us. He knows us far better than we could ever imagine and because he knows us so well, we can only become truly happy, free, fulfilled and at peace by following his will for our lives. "I came so that they might have life and have it more abundantly." (John 10:10).

In order to have life in its fullest, each of us needs to make a decision to have a personal relationship with Jesus Christ. When we say "yes" to knowing Christ personally and then put our lives at his disposal we will enjoy peace in this world and in the world to come.

GROWING IN YOUR PERSONAL RELATIONSHIP
WITH JESUS CHRIST

"The Liturgy of the Word helps us to know Jesus Christ better. Not just know about him, but to know him. The really good news is that Jesus wants you to know him better and to grow in friendship with him. He speaks to you through the Liturgy of the Word" (Fr. David Scotchie, "Jesus wants you to know him better", *The Florida Catholic*, Jan 14-27, 2011).

Our participation in the Sacraments (especially Eucharist) also helps us develop a closer relationship with Christ. He invites us to unite ourselves to him in his Sacrifice on Calvary and to carry his Word in our actions every day. In every Mass we are reminded that Jesus asks us for the highest form of worship— to imitate him and be "light for the world" (Matthew 5:16).

We can also know Christ better when we pray daily, read the Bible regularly and when we participate in small group studies such as *Navigating Your Finances God's Way* in community with others.

GOD LOVES YOU AND WANTS YOU TO KNOW HIM

God created people in his own image, and he desires a close relationship with each of us. My friend directed my attention to two passages: "For God so loved the world, that he gave His only Son, so that everyone who believes in him might not perish, but might have eternal life" (John 3:16). ". . . I [Jesus] came that they might have life and have it more abundantly" (John 10:10).

When Howard's son, Matthew, was in the first grade, he developed a burning desire to win the 100-yard dash at his school's field day. That was all the family heard about for two months. But there was a problem: his classmate Bobby Dike was faster than Matthew.

Field day finally arrived. They ran the 50-yard dash first, and Bobby easily beat Matthew. Howard will never forget when Matthew came up to me with tears in his eyes, pleading, "Daddy, please pray for me in the 100-yard dash. I've just got to win." Howard's heart sank as he nodded.

With the sound of the gun, Matthew got off to a quick start. Halfway through the race he pulled away from the rest of his classmates and won. Howard lost control of himself! He was jumping and shouting. He had never before experienced such exhilaration. Then it occurred to him how much he loved his son. Although Howard loves other people, he doesn't love them enough to give his son to die for them. But that is how much God the Father loved you. He gave his only Son, Jesus Christ, to die for you.

CONTRAST

Society Says: God is irrelevant.

Scripture Says: God is essential.

COMMITMENT

Strengthen your relationship with Jesus Christ by attending Mass on a regular basis.

THIRTEEN

CHILDREN

The ABC's of Money

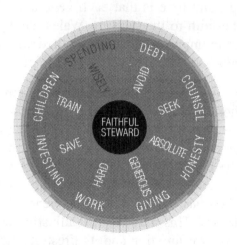

Learning to handle money one step at a time is part of a child's education, a part that parents cannot leave to teachers but must direct themselves. Spending experiences are found in the outside world rather than in the classroom.

Howard and Bev met the Hitchcock family at the park for a picnic. As they watched their children play, Jean expressed a concern. "Allen and I were not trained by our parents to handle money responsibly, and I'm afraid we're not doing a much better job. Our children just don't understand the value of money. What should we do?"

This is a question all parents need to answer.

In 1904 the country of Wales experienced a remarkable revival. Thousands of people became Christians, and the results were dramatic. Bars closed because of a lack of business. Policemen exchanged their weapons for white gloves as crime disappeared. Horses didn't understand their drivers because profanities were no longer uttered. Wales sent missionaries all over the world.

By the early 1970s things had changed drastically in Wales. Less than one half of one percent of the Welsh attended church. Divorce was at an all-time high, and the crime rate was escalating rapidly. Many churches had closed and had been converted to bars, and rugby had replaced Christianity as the national religion.

The key learning point here is that each generation is responsible for passing on the faith to the next. In Wales, despite tremendous spiritual vitality, the impact of Christianity had all but disappeared in 70 years. Parents had failed to pass their faith on to their children.

> Parents have work of great importance to do in the domestic church, the home. Within the family, they must teach their children the truths of the faith and pray with them; share Christian values with them in the face of pressures to conform to the hostile values of a secularized society; and initiate them into the practice of stewardship itself, in all its dimensions, contrary to today's widespread consumerism and individualism. This may require adjusting the family's own patterns of consumption and its lifestyle, including the use of television, internet and other media which sometimes preach values in conflict with the mind of Christ. Above all, it requires that parents themselves be models of stewardship especially by their selfless service to one another, to their children, and to church and community needs (*Stewardship: A Disciple's Response,* USCCB, 32).

Answer this question: When you left home, how well prepared were you to make financial decisions? Parents and teachers spend 18 to 22 years preparing youth for occupations but generally less than a few hours teaching children the value and use of the money they will earn during their careers.

MVP PARENTS

Parents should be MVP parents. MVP is an acronym that describes the three methods to teach children God's way of handling money: Modeling, Verbal communication, and Practical opportunities. All three are needed to train your children. Let's look at each.

Modeling

Since children soak up parental attitudes toward money like a sponge soaks up water, parents must model handling money wisely. Paul recognized the importance of example when he said, "Imitate me, then, just as I imitate Christ" (1 Corinthians 11:1, GNT). The Lord used this strategy. He sent the perfect model, Jesus Christ, to demonstrate how we should live.

Luke 6:40 (GNT) is a challenging passage. It reads, "No pupils are greater than their teacher; but all pupils, when they have completed their training, will be like their teacher." Another way of saying this is that we can teach what we believe, but we only reproduce who we are. There is no substitute for parents being good models.

Verbal Communication

Parents need to tell their children why they are handling money the way they are. The Lord charged the Israelites, "Never forget these commands that I am giving you today. Teach them to your children. Repeat them when you are at home and when you are away, when you are resting and when you are working" (Deuteronomy 6:6-7, GNT). We must verbally instruct our children in the ways of the Lord, but children need more than mere verbal instruction; they also need a practical experience.

Practical Experiences

Children then need to be given opportunities to apply what they have heard and seen. There are learning experiences which benefit the child in the area of money management (the art of wise spending) and money making (the value of work).

LEARNING EXPERIENCES IN
"MONEY MANAGEMENT"

As soon as children are ready for school, they should begin to receive an income to manage. Parents need to decide whether the children must earn an income, or if they wish to give an allowance in return for the children doing chores.

The amount of the income will vary according to such factors as the child's age and ability to earn. However, the amount is not as important as the responsibility of handling money. At first it is a new experience, and the child will make many mistakes. Don't hesitate to let the "law of natural consequences" run its course. You're going to be tempted to help little Johnny when he spends all his income the first day on an unwise purchase. You won't like the fact that he has to live the rest of the week without all the other things he wants and maybe needs. Don't bail him out. His mistakes will be his best teacher.

Parents should establish boundaries and offer advice on how to spend money, but your child must have freedom of choice. Excessive restrictions will only reduce his opportunities to learn by experience. The first few pennies and nickels will make a lasting impression. Every Saturday morning Howard used to bicycle to the store with his son Matthew to buy him a pack of his favorite gum. Despite Howard's persistent advice, the entire pack would be consumed that first day.

When Matthew started to receive income, Howard and Bev decided that he would have to buy his own gum. Howard will never forget the pained look on Matthew's face as he came out of the store with his first purchase. "Daddy, this gum cost me all my money," he blurted. That pack was rationed with tender care and lasted more than a week.

Parents should slowly increase the income as the child grows in his ability and demonstrates wise spending patterns.

Budgeting

When children begin to receive an income, teach them how to budget. Begin with a simple system consisting of three jars, each labeled by category—give, save and spend. The child distributes a portion of his income into each jar. Thus, a simple budget is established using visual control. When the jar is empty, there is no money to spend. Even a six-year-old can understand this method.

By the time children are 12, they are old enough to be exposed to the family's budget. They will understand that they are growing up, because they can now share in making plans for spending the family income. They will realize that each member has a responsibility for wise spending, regardless of who provides the income. As children mature, they should participate in every aspect of the family budget. It will help them to realize the extent and limitations of the family income as well as how to make the money stretch to meet the family's needs.

At first a child may think that the family has so much money that it is impossible to spend it all. To help her visualize the budget, using play money, have the family income converted to a stack of dollars. Place these on a table and divide the "income" pile into the various "expense" piles representing the categories of spending. It is often difficult for children to grasp numbers because they are abstract. The dollars will provide a tangible way for a child to understand the family budget.

During the budget training, teach your child to become a wise consumer. Teach shopping skills, the ability to distinguish needs from wants and the fine art of waiting on the Lord to provide. Warn the child about the powerful influence of advertising and the danger of impulse spending.

When the child becomes a teenager, discontinue the allowance unless he presents a budget that accounts for how the last week's allowance was spent.

Giving

The best time to establish the personal habit of giving is when you are young. It is helpful for children to give a portion of their gifts to a tangible need they can visualize. For example, a child can understand the impact of his gift when his contribution is helping to construct the new church building or when it is buying food for a needy family he knows.

Dr. Richard Halverson, former chaplain of the U.S. Senate, gave his son Chris this rich heritage as a child. Through a ministry that serves poor children, Chris and his brother gave money to support a Korean orphan named Kim who had lost his sight and an arm during the Korean War. Chris was taught to feel that Kim was his adopted brother. One Christmas, Chris bought Kim a harmonica. It was Kim's first personal possession. He cherished this gift from Chris and learned to play it well. Today Kim is an evangelist, and in his presentation of the gospel he includes playing the harmonica. By being trained to give as a youth, Chris experienced firsthand the value of meeting people's needs and seeing God change lives as a result of faithful giving.

When your child is a teenager, a family or church mission trip to a developing country or serving in an disadvantaged urban setting can be a powerful experience. Direct exposure to these types of situations can provide great lessons in social justice issues and can initiate a lifetime of giving to the poor.

We also recommend a special family time each week for dedicating that week's gifts to the Lord. It is important for the children to participate in this time of dedication and worship. The more involved children are with their parents in the proper handling of money, the better habits they will have as adults.

Saving and Investing

The habit of saving should be established as soon as the child receives an income. It is helpful to open a savings account for your child at this time. As the child matures, you also should expose him or her to various types of investments—stocks, bonds, real estate, etc.

Teach your children the benefits of compounding. If they grasp this concept and become faithful savers, they will enjoy more financial stability as adults. Parents should demonstrate saving by doing so for something that will directly benefit the children. A good example is a family vacation. Use a graph the children can fill in so they can chart the progress of the family's saving for a vacation.

Children should have both short-term and long-term saving programs. The younger the child, the more important are short-term achievable goals. To a four-year-old, a week seems like a lifetime to save for a small purchase. He or she will not understand about saving for future education or retirement but will get excited about saving for a small toy. For older children, long-term saving for education, the first car, etc. should be a requirement. Some parents find it motivating to their child if they match their child's contribution to their long-term savings.

Debt

It is also important to teach the cost of money and how difficult it is to get out of debt. Dick Getty loaned his son and daughter the money to buy bicycles. Dick drew up a credit agreement with a schedule for repayment of the loan. He included the interest charged. After they successfully went through the long, difficult process of paying off the loan, the family celebrated with a "mortgage burning" ceremony. Dick said that his children have appreciated those bikes more than any of their other possessions, and they have vowed to avoid debt in the future.

LEARNING EXPERIENCE IN "MONEY MAKING"

Because work is an essential element in becoming a faithful steward, parents have the responsibility to train each child in the value of work and proper work habits. If a child responds and learns how to work with a proper attitude, then he or she will not only have taken a giant step to becoming content, but he or she will become a valuable commodity in the job market. Clearly, children need to learn the dignity and the habit of work. There are four areas to consider in this training.

Establish routine responsibilities

The best way for a child to become faithful in work is to establish the habit of daily household chores. For example, Howard's daughter carried out the garbage and washed the dishes, and his son cleaned the floors.

Expose your children to your work

Not too many years ago most children were active participants in earning the family's money. They readily learned responsibility and the value of money. However, that is seldom the case today. Many children don't know how their father or mother earns the family income.

During a class several years ago, a participant said that he had asked his father what he did at work. "I make money," the father had responded. "For a long time I thought my dad actually made dollar bills. My mother would ask Dad, 'How much did you draw this week?' I thought he was a great artist to be able to do all that detailed lettering and artwork."

An important way to teach the value of work is to expose the child to the parents' means of earning a living. If your children cannot visit you at work, at least take the time to explain your job to them. For those parents who manage their own businesses, children should be encouraged to participate.

One word of advice: because most children are no longer with their parents at work, the parents' work attitudes and habits around the home will be a major modeling influence. If a parent works hard at the office but complains about washing the dishes at home, what's being communicated to the children about work? Examine your work attitudes and activities at home to ensure that you are properly influencing your children to be godly workers.

Earn extra money at home

You should encourage your child to do extra work to earn money. A good rule of thumb is to pay the child a fair wage for the work you would have to hire someone to do. For example, if your car needs washing and your daughter needs some extra money and wants to wash it, let her. Be happy to pay her rather than the person at the car wash.

Encourage your child to work for others

A babysitting job, janitorial work, lawn care or waiting tables will serve as an education. A job gives a child an opportunity to enter into an employee-employer relationship and to earn extra money.

As your child enters high school it is a good idea to discontinue allowances during summer vacation. This will motivate him to earn his own money by holding a summer job. Moreover, some students can handle part-time work during the school year.

The objective of training your children in the value of work is to build and discipline their character. A working child with the proper attitude will be a more satisfied individual. They will grow up with more respect for the value of money and what is required to earn it.

DEPENDENCE AND DANGER

Fathers in our country spend less time with their children than fathers in almost every other nation of the world. Fathers currently spend an average of less than three minutes a day communicating with their sons. In the Bible, David and Eli were both godly men who had remarkably productive careers. Yet both lost sons through careless fathering.

If children are going to thrive, it will be because parents place them high on their list of priorities, consistently reserving adequate time and energy for leadership within their homes. Fathers, we plead with you to seize the opportunity to train your children. You are literally influencing generations.

It is very common these days for a single mother to be the head of the household. We appreciate the demands these mothers face. But please be encouraged. Some of the most responsible children we have ever met have been raised by godly single mothers.

Dependence on Prayer

One of the most valuable lessons you can teach your children is to pray for the Lord's guidance and provision. The Lord wants to demonstrate that he is actively involved in each of our lives. One way he does this is by answering our prayers. Because of our affluent society, we often rob ourselves of this opportunity. We can buy things or charge purchases without prayerfully allowing the Lord to supply them. We need to be creative in how we can experience the reality of God in the area of our spending, and we need to be careful to communicate that value to our children.

Danger of Overindulgence

When it comes to money, parents are always on a tightrope trying to keep a proper balance. They can easily be too miserly with money. In our affluent culture, however, they are more often overindulgent, and consequently hamper the development of their children's character. Clearly, overindulgence with money can retard the development of a child's character and destroy the need for initiative and motivation. Too often it creates in a child a constant expectation to be given things without having to work or save for them.

STRATEGY FOR INDEPENDENCE

Finally, we need to establish a strategy for independence. Lyle and Marge have four extremely mature and responsible children. Their strategy has been to work toward having each child independently managing all of his or her own finances (with the exception of food and shelter) by the senior year in high school. In this way they could be available to advise the children as they learn to make spending decisions.

Let's review how MVP parents train their children:

1. **Model financial faithfulness**, allowing your children to observe closely how you apply these principles.

2. **Verbally communicate** Gods way of handling money.

3. **Create practical opportunities** for your children to experience God's financial principles. Each child has an individual personality and temperament. One child may spend wildly yet be very generous; another may save everything and never want to give. Study your children's personality carefully and tailor the training to fit the child.

As the country of Wales discovered, God has no grandchildren. Passing on our faith in Christ to the next generation can be compared to a relay race. Any track coach will tell you that relay races are often won or lost in the passing of the baton from one runner to another. Seldom is the baton dropped once it is firmly in the grasp of a runner. If it is going to be dropped, it is in the exchange that takes place between the runners. As parents, we have the responsibility to pass the baton of practical biblical truths to our children. At times during the training it may seem as if there is little progress. Nonetheless, be consistent and persistent!

I have yet to meet an adult whose parents lived all of these biblical financial principles and taught them systematically to their children. As an unfortunate consequence of this lack of training, children have left home ill-equipped to manage their financial future according to Scripture. I pray our generation will leave our children the blessed legacy of financial faithfulness.

CONTRAST

Society says: Parents need not require their children to establish the discipline of managing money or of working hard.

Scripture says: Parents have the obligation to train a child to be a faithful steward, a wise money manager and a hard worker.

COMMITMENT

Evaluate what your children are learning about work and handling money.

FOURTEEN

BUDGET

Keep Abreast of the Facts

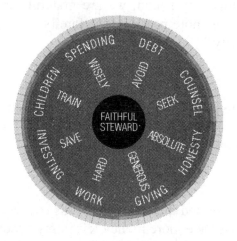

The day Howard and Bev went to see Jean Hitchcock's parents, Frank and Vivian Webster, there was not even a hint of what they had gone through the previous year. For the Websters it had been a year of dramatic upheaval. Frank had suffered a stroke that paralyzed his left side and caused him to lose his job. They were forced to sell their cozy lakefront home and readjust to a much lower standard of living.

The clean, neat apartment they now called home was sparsely furnished. It was apparent that they were going through hard times. Vivian explained their readjustment. "We have been amazed at what we can live without. We have been forced to watch every penny and follow a strict budget."

Their backs were against a financial wall, and the Websters had responded by economizing at every turn. They went without air-conditioning, no longer ate at restaurants and limited the use of the hot water heater to 30 minutes a day—just enough for showers and the dishes. Their conservation was paying off. They were actually putting more money into savings than when they were living on Frank's lucrative salary as an engineer. However, during those years of easy spending, they had lived without the restraints of a budget.

"The trauma of unemployment forced us to communicate in an area of our lives that had been 'off limits' during the 'good old days,'" Vivian explained. "We have learned more about each other through this adversity than at any other time during our 37 years of marriage. As strange as this may sound, we are grateful that this hardship happened. There is more peace in our family now than during the years of prosperity."

WHAT IS A BUDGET?

The Websters are proof that when we plan where our money is to go, we can make the money go further. That's what a budget is—a plan for spending money.

WHY BUDGET?

When the bank notified the depositor of his overdraft he replied in disbelief, "I must have more money left in my account. I still have six checks in my checkbook!" Like the surprised depositor, if you do not have a written budget, chances are that you are flying by the seat of your financial pants.

Budgeting is not always fun, but it is the only way to follow through and apply what has been learned about getting out of debt, saving and giving. Regardless of income, most of us have difficulty making ends meet unless there is a plan for spending. It seems that there is "too much month at the end of the money" unless a planned and disciplined approach to spending is followed.

Budgeting provides an opportunity to pray about spending decisions

This is important because according to a survey of young husbands, more than 50 percent of the most serious marital problems are financial. In fact, one judge has said, "Quarreling about money is the major reason for our unprecedented divorce rate." I seldom see a family with financial problems where there is not real tension within the marriage.

A successful budget should be a team effort. It is a good communication tool for the husband and wife to use. A budget also can help a family get full value for its money without losing sight of the things its members want most.

A family in our neighborhood is committed to sending their children to camp each summer for two weeks. Several years ago as they were planning their annual budget in January, it became apparent that there would not be enough money for the children to go to camp. The family then agreed each member would "contribute" to summer camp by making a sacrifice: the father gave up his golf game once a month, the mother did not join her summer bowling league and the children received half their normal allowance. By using a budget, the family was able to anticipate a problem and adjust their spending to enable them to get what they wanted most, in this case, summer camp.

HOW TO BUDGET

A budget is useful only if it is used. It should be a plan tailor-made for managing your finances, not someone else's. Some people are more comfortable using a handwritten process, while others prefer using budget software or an online budget.

To set up your budget, follow these three steps:

1. Begin where you are today.

Developing a budget must begin with the current situation. Determine how much money is earned and spent. Most people do not know what they are actually earning and spending. For this reason it is essential to keep a record of every penny for a month to get an accurate picture in order to complete an estimated budget.

If your wages are not the same each month (like the income of a commissioned salesperson), make a conservative estimate of your annual income by adding your income during the past 12 months, subtracting the highest month, and dividing by 11 to establish a working figure for your monthly bugetary income.

Now determine which expenses do not occur each month. Examples are real estate taxes and vacations. Estimate how much you spend for these each year and divide that amount by 12 to determine your monthly cost. Armed with this information, you can complete the Estimated Monthly Budget on the next page. Do not be discouraged. Almost every budget starts out with expenditures in excess of income. But there is hope!

2. The solution is where you want to be.

To solve the problem of spending more than you earn, you must either increase your income or decrease your expenditures. It is that simple. Either earn more or spend less. There are no other alternatives.

Adding to Your Income

A part-time job, or better yet, a project that would involve the whole family, will increase your income. The ever-present danger of increasing income is the tendency for expenses also to rise. To avoid this problem agree ahead of time to apply any extra income to balancing the budget.

Reducing Expenses

Howard's father was in the hotel business when he was growing up. He owned a small resort in Florida that catered to tourists. Business was seasonal; during the winter it flourished, but in the summer it withered to almost nothing. Just the thought of summer sent chills down his spine, but after the lean months he was always grateful. Summer taught him the habit of asking these questions about his expenses: Which are absolutely necessary? Which can I do without? Which can I reduce?

You can ask these same questions of your personal budget as you work to reduce spending.

Annual income twenty pounds,
Annual expenditure nineteen six,
Result happiness

Annual income twenty pounds,
Annual expenditure twenty
pounds ought and six, Result
misery.

—Charles Dickens

---

3. Do not stop!

The most common temptation is to stop budgeting. Don't do it. Frankly, many people find it difficult to begin a budget by themselves. If you have not yet enrolled in the Compass small group study, we challenge you to do so. In the small group environment you will be encouraged yet held accountable to implement biblical financial principles.

Remember, a budget is simply a plan for spending your money. It will not work by itself. Every area of your budget should be regularly reviewed to keep a rein on spending. "By wisdom a house is built, by understanding it is made firm; And by knowledge its rooms are filled with every precious and pleasing possession" (Proverbs 24:3-4).

Through the years there will be frustrations, but a budget, if properly used, will save you thousands of dollars. It will help you accumulate savings and will help you stay out of debt. More importantly, it will help husbands and wives communicate in an area that is a leading cause of marital conflict.

Please review the sample budget, percentage guidelilnes, budget descriptions and hints on the following pages as you prepare to create your own budget.

ESTIMATED MONTHLY BUDGET

GROSS MONTHLY INCOME		7. CLOTHING	
SALARY		Adults	
INTEREST		Children	
DIVIDENDS		Cleaning	
OTHER INCOME		**8. MEDICAL & HEALTH**	
LESS		Doctor	
1. GIVING		Dentist	
2. TAXES (FED.,STATE, FICA)		Prescriptions	
NET SPENDABLE INCOME		Vision/Dental	
LIVING EXPENSES		Disability	
3. SAVING & INVESTING		Long Term Care	
Emergency Savings		**9. EDUCATION**	
Auto Replacement		Adult Education	
401k/403b/Retirement		Kid's tuition/Supplies	
College Funds		Tutoring/Activities	
IRA		**10. PERSONAL**	
4. HOUSING		Allowances	
Mortgage or Rent		Childcare/Babysitting	
Insurance		Life Insurance	
Property Taxes		Toiletries	
Electricity		Gifts	
Heating/Gas		Pets	
Water		Sports/Hobbies	
Sanitation		Subscriptions/Dues	
Telephone		**11. ENTERTAINMENT/VACATIONS**	
Maintenance		Activities	
Cleaning & Supplies		Vacations/Travel	
Other		Videos/Books/Music	
5. FOOD		**12. DEBTS**	
6. TRANSPORTATION			
Auto Payments		**TOTAL LIVING EXPENSES**	
Gas & Oil		**INCOME VS. LIVING EXPENSES**	
Insurance		**LESS TOTAL LIVING EXPENSES**	
Repairs/Maint./Replace		**SURPLUS OR DEFICIT**	
Other			

Here are some guidelines to help you evaluate your major expenses. Actual percentages may vary depending upon the cost of housing where you live, the size of your family and your income. When you exceed the upper range in a category, this should warn you to carefully evaluate your spending in that category.

PERCENTAGE GUIDELINE

Category	Percent of Income (after giving and taxes)
Savings & Investing	5-15%
Housing	30-40%
Food	5-15%
Transportation	10-15%
Clothing	2-7%
Medical / Health	5-10%
Education	2-7%
Personal	5-10%
Entertainment / Vacation	5-10%
Debts	0-10%

Consider these suggestions to spend more wisely:

Shelter

1. Purchase an older house that you can improve with your own labor. You can also buy a modest-size house suitable to your needs today with a design that can be expanded to meet your future needs.

2. Consider renting. It can be less expensive than owning and involves fewer responsibilities—lawn care, maintenance, etc.

3. If you can do repair and maintenance work such as lawn care, pest control, painting and carpet cleaning, you will save a substantial amount.

4. Lower the cost of utilities by limiting the use of heating, air conditioning, lights and appliances.

5. Shop carefully for furniture and appliances. Garage sales are a good source for reasonably priced household goods.

Food

1. Prepare a menu for the week. Then list the ingredients from the menu and shop according to the list. This will help you plan a nutritionally balanced diet, avoid impulse shopping and eliminate waste.

2. Shop once a week. Each time we go shopping for "some little thing," we always buy "some other little thing" as well.

3. Cut out the ready-to-eat food, which has expensive labor added to the price.

4. Leave children and hungry spouses at home when shopping. The fewer distractions from the list the better.

5. Lunches eaten out are often budget breakers. A lunch prepared at home and taken to work will help the budget and the waistline.

6. Reduce the use of paper products. Paper plates, cups and napkins are expensive to use.

Transportation

1. If you have two cars, try to get by with one, this will be the biggest transportation savings.

2. Purchase a low-cost used car and drive it until repairs become too expensive.

3. The smaller the car, the more economical to operate. You pay an estimated 35 cents a pound each year to operate an automobile.

Clothing

1. Make a written list of yearly clothing needs. Shop from the list during the off-season sales at economical clothing stores and at garage sales.

2. Purchase simple basic fashions that stay in style longer than faddish clothes.

3. Do not purchase a lot of clothing. Select one or two basic colors for your wardrobe, and buy outfits that you can wear in combination with others.

4. Purchase home-washable fabrics. Clothes that must be commercially cleaned are expensive to maintain.

Insurance

1. Select insurance based on your need and budget, and secure estimates from three major insurance companies.

2. Raising the deductible feature will substantially reduce premiums.

3. Seek the recommendation of friends for a skilled insurance agent. A capable agent can save you money.

Health

1. Practice preventive medicine. Your body will stay healthier when you get the proper amount of sleep, exercise and nutrition.

2. Practice proper oral hygiene for healthy teeth and to reduce dental bills.

3. Ask friends to recommend reasonable and competent physicians and dentists.

Entertainment and Recreation

1. Plan your vacation for the off-season and select destinations near home.

2. Rather than expensive entertainment, seek creative alternatives such as picnics or exploring free state parks.

Five Budgeting Hints

1. Reconcile your bank statement each month.

2. It is helpful to have a separate savings account where you can deposit the monthly allotment for the bills that do not come due each month. For example, if your annual insurance premium is $960, deposit $80 in this savings account each month. This ensures the money will be available when these payments come due.

3. We are trained to think monthly. To better understand the impact of an expense, figure the yearly cost. For example, if you spend $6 for lunch each working day, multiply $6 by five days a week by 50 weeks a year. It totals $1,500 for lunches. Thinking yearly shows the true cost of seemingly inconsequential expenses.

4. Control impulse spending. Impulse spending ranges from buying big things like automobiles to small items like tools. Each time you have the urge to spend for something not planned, post it to an "wish list" and pray about the purchase for several days. As you do this, the impulse will often pass.

5. It is wise for husbands and wives to include personal allowances in the budget. Both should be given allowances to spend as they please. The husband and wife can participate in their favorite activities so long as their allowance permits. This will eliminate many arguments.

CONTRAST

Society Says: Budgeting is painful and unnecessary.

Scripture Says: Good stewards are required to manage money and possessions faithfully.

COMMITMENT

Keep a careful record of all expenditures for 30-60 days to determine your current situation. After that, plan a budget suited to your income and personal objectives. Put it into effect.

FIFTEEN

STANDARD OF LIVING

How Shall We Then Live?

Howard was invited to attend the second anniversary of a very special event, the day the Hitchcocks reached their goal of becoming debt-free. Two years later they were just as grateful for their new freedom and, more importantly, their marriage was growing stronger. Although it had been a struggle for them, and several times they had been on the verge of quitting, the stakes of saving their marriage were too high. They persevered and reached their goal.

Allen and Jean were now facing a new challenge: their income now exceeded their expenses. How should they spend the surplus? They had major decisions to make. Should they move to a larger home or stay in their present one and work on paying off the mortgage? Should they purchase a new car? Should they adopt a more expensive lifestyle or continue to save and give more?

The Bible does not dictate one particular standard of living for everyone. However, Scripture contains a number of challenging principles that we should consider when choosing a lifestyle.

THINK WITH AN ETERNAL PERSPECTIVE

Nurture an eternal perspective. Our culture and the media implore us to focus on the immediate. Advertisers persuade consumers to gratify themselves today with no thought of tomorrow. Examine the following to understand how brief life is on earth compared with eternity:

ETERNITY PAST   ETERNITY FUTURE

Our momentary time on earth is but a dot on the timeline of eternity. Yet we have the opportunity to influence eternity by how we handle money today. We have not only the privilege to lay up treasures for ourselves in heaven but also the opportunity to spend money to influence people for Jesus Christ. Gaining eternal perspective and eternal values will have a profound effect on your decision-making.

Moses is a good example. Study Hebrews 11:24-26 carefully: "By faith Moses, when he had grown up, refused to be known as the son of Pharaoh's daughter; he chose to be ill-treated along with the people of God rather than enjoy the fleeting pleasure of sin. He considered the reproach of the Anointed greater wealth than the treasures of Egypt, for he was looking to the recompense."

Moses faced a choice. As Pharaoh's adopted son he could enjoy the lavish lifestyle of royalty, or he could choose to become a Hebrew slave. Because he had an eternal perspective, he chose the latter and was used by the Lord in a remarkable way. We face a similar decision. We can either live with a view toward eternity or live focused on this present world.

Have you ever returned as an adult to a place you knew as a child? Howard once visited a field on which he played as a 12 year old. He remembered it as a huge field surrounded by towering fences and was shocked to discover how small it really was! Or do you remember wanting to get something so much you could almost taste it? Yet today it means almost nothing to you. We will experience something similar when we arrive in heaven. Many things that seem so important to us now will fade into insignificance in the light of eternity.

You are a pilgrim

Scripture tells us about our identity and role on earth: First of all, "We . . . are citizens of heaven," (Philippians 3:20 GNT). Second, "We are ambassadors for Christ" (2 Corinthians 5:20). Third, we are aliens, strangers and pilgrims on this earth (Cf. Hebrews 11:13).

Peter wrote, ". . . spend the rest of your lives here on earth in reverence for him [Jesus]" (1 Peter 1:17, GNT). Later he added, "I urge you as strangers and sojourners to keep away from worldly desires that wage war against the soul" (1 Peter 2:11).

The Catholic Church refers to itself as the "pilgrim Church on earth". A pilgrim is a traveler and not a settler—one who is acutely aware that the excessive accumulation of things can only distract from reaching the goal or destination. Material possessions are valuable to a pilgrim only as they facilitate his mission. The pilgrim is a traveler who chooses possessions strategically, regarding most of them as encumbrances that would slow the journey or make it impossible. Of course, many become "settlers" in the temporal sense, living in houses and owning furniture and developing businesses. There is nothing wrong with this, but we need to maintain a pilgrim mentality of detachment—the traveler's philosophy of traveling light.

Acquire only those possessions that enable you to fulfill God's calling on your life.

Make an effort to live simply

Every possession requires time, attention and often money to maintain it. Too many or the wrong types of possessions can demand so much time, energy or money that they harm our relationship with the Lord and others. The quiet, simple life is the best environment to allow us enough time to nurture our relationship with the Lord. "We must live simply so that others may simply live" (St. Elizabeth Ann Seton).

We are at war

"Bear your share of hardship along with me like a good soldier of Christ Jesus. To satisfy the one who recruited him, a soldier does not become entangled in the business affairs of life" (2 Timothy 2:3-4). In wartime, people often alter their lifestyles radically to help win the war. They ration the use of strategically important items. They spend less on life's comforts so that the army will be adequately supplied. As soldiers, we should be careful not to become unduly encumbered with the cares of this life.

Recognize the enemy

"For our struggle is not against flesh and blood, but with . . . the evil spirits in the heavens" (Ephesians 6:12). In a war you are going to use your most effective weapon. The devil's mission is to divert us from serving Christ. He frequently accomplishes this by tempting us to serve money and possessions. As we have seen before, money is the primary competitor with Christ for the lordship of our life. "You cannot serve God and mammon [money]" (Matthew 6:24).

Serving money is often difficult to identify because loving money is a respectable sin—people will congratulate you for acquiring the trappings of financial success. Therefore, you should prayerfully examine your relationship with Christ and money.

Spend in a way that pleases the Lord

Prayerfully submit spending decisions to the Lord. Everything we possess is owned by the Lord, and we should spend to please him and not for a selfish purpose. Seeking the Lord's direction in spending does not mean that we will never spend for anything other than a basic necessity. Recreation, appropriate leisure activities and rest are important. "For everything created by God is good, and nothing is to be rejected when received with thanksgiving" (1 Timothy 4:4).

Do not compare yourself to others

Some use comparison to justify spending more than they should. Many have suffered financially because they tried but could not afford to "keep up with the Joneses." Someone once said, "You can never keep up with the Joneses. Just about the time you catch them, they refinance their home and go deeper in debt to buy more things!" If you are wealthy, your lifestyle should be based on the conviction that the Lord wants you to have a certain standard of living, which is not necessarily dictated by the maximum you can afford.

If only I had more . . .

Have you ever felt that if only you were in a more prestigious position or had more money, then you could accomplish really significant things for the Lord?

Let's examine two men who lived in Rome and were at different ends of the economic spectrum. Before gladiator contests in the coliseum, everyone would stand, waiting silently for Caesar. The contests could not begin until he arrived. When Caesar arrived, he was greeted with thunderous shouts of "Hail Caesar!" He had more power, prestige and wealth than anyone else living at that time. He was worshiped as though he were a god.

Elsewhere in Rome was another man in vastly different circumstances. He was in prison. He invested his time praying and writing to his friends. His name was Paul.

One man lived in an opulent palace. The other lived in a dingy cell. One had almost unlimited wealth. The other had almost nothing. One was the center of attention. The other was virtually ignored. Almost 2,000 years later, people around the world recognize which of these two men made the eternally important contribution. They name their children after the prisoner and their salads after the emperor!

Being used by Christ in a significant way has nothing to do with a high position or great riches. It has everything to do with a willingness to allow Christ to become your Lord.

Do not be conformed to this world

Romans 12:2 (GNT) begins with this command: "Do not conform yourselves to the standards of this world, but let God transform you inwardly by a complete change of your mind. Then you will be able to know the will of God—what is good and pleasing to him and is perfect."

We live in one of the most affluent cultures the world has ever known. And we are constantly bombarded with costly, manipulative advertising whose purpose is to prompt us to spend money. Advertisers usually stress the importance of image rather than function. For example, automobile ads rarely focus on a car as reliable transportation that is economical to operate; instead, an image of status or sex appeal is projected.

Reflect on the claims of TV commercials. No matter what the product—clothing, deodorants, credit cards, cars, beverages, you name it—the message is communicated that the "fulfilling, beautiful, wrinkle-free life" can be ours if we are willing to buy it. Unfortunately, this media onslaught has influenced all of us to some extent. George Fooshee, the author of the excellent book You Can Beat the Money Squeeze, so aptly states, "People buy things they do not need with money they do not have to impress people they do not even like." [6]

> *Let temporal things serve your use, but the eternal be the object of your desire.*
>
> —Thomas á Kempis

The following graph depicts how the artificial, media-generated lifestyle influences our lives. The bottom curve represents our income—what we really can afford to buy. The next curve illustrates how much we actually spend. We make up the difference between our income and spending by the use of debt, which creates slavery, financial pressure and anxiety. The top of the graph demonstrates what advertisers tell us to buy. It's an image-conscious, expensive lifestyle that claims to satisfy the human heart's deepest needs. When we want to live this counterfeit, media-induced dream but cannot afford it, we suffer discontent, envy and coveting.

None of us is immune to the lure of this message. Several years ago a sharp-looking van in a television commercial caught Howard's eye. Their family had a second-hand, 11-year-old station wagon painted an unattractive yellow. This advertised van was perfect—just the right size and color. Howard even rationalized that this van would be better suited for use in ministry. He found himself spending half an hour each day studying beautiful, slick brochures, admiring new vans on the highway and day-dreaming about driving one. He was hooked! The yellow station wagon seemed to get more unsightly every day, while the van went from an "I want it" to an "I need it" category.

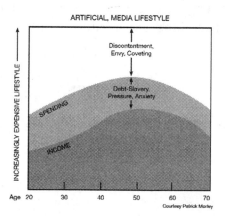

Howard was about to buy the van when he decided to seek the counsel of Jack Norman, a local car dealer and friend. He gave Howard good advice. He asked him how many miles the station wagon had been driven. "Fifty-five thousand miles," Howard responded. Jack thought for a moment and then he said, "The station wagon is in good condition and should be great transportation for years!" Howard didn't want to hear that, but reluctantly agreed with him.

Jack's advice had saved Howard thousands of dollars. Moreover, the moment the decision was made to keep the yellow station wagon, Howard lost the desire for the van. It no longer dominated his thinking. Interestingly enough, the yellow station wagon had become better-looking!

From time to time we all get hooked on something we think we must buy—a car, home, camera, boat, you name it. Once hooked, it's easy to rationalize a purchase. Please remember to seek the Lord's guidance and the counsel of godly people when making spending decisions.

CONTRAST

Society says: Acquire as many expensive possessions as possible because they are evidence you are a successful, important person.

Scripture says: The excessive accumulation of possessions will distract you from fulfilling God's purpose for your life.

COMMITMENT

I will prayerfully determine what standard of living the Lord wants for me.

SIXTEEN

PERSPECTIVE

What's Really Important

A young Roger Morgan came out of the Appalachian Mountains with the sole purpose of making a fortune. Money became his god, and he became worth millions. Then the stock market crash of 1929 and the Great Depression reduced him to utter poverty. Penniless, he took to the road. One day a friend found him on the Golden Gate Bridge staring down into the waters of the San Francisco Bay, and he suggested they move on. "Leave me alone," Roger replied. "I'm trying to think. There is something more important than money, but I've forgotten what it is."

What Roger Morgan forgot, or perhaps never knew, was the scriptural perspective of money. That is what we will explore in this chapter.

MONEY WILL NOT BRING TRUE HAPPINESS

King Solomon had an annual income of more than $25 million. He lived in a palace that took 13 years to build. He owned 40,000 stalls of horses. He sat on an ivory throne over-laid with gold. He drank from gold cups. The daily menu of his household included 100 sheep and 30 oxen in addition to deer and fowl (See 1 Kings 5:1 — 1 Kings 7:1).

Obviously, Solomon was in a position to know whether money would bring happiness, and he didn't hesitate to say that riches do not bring true happiness: "If you love money, you will never be satisfied; if you long to be rich, you will never get all you want. It is useless. The richer you are, the more mouths you have to feed. All you gain is the knowledge that you are rich" (Ecclesiastes 5:10-11, GNT).

In contrast, most people believe you can buy happiness. The American Institute of Public Opinion found that 70 percent of Americans thought they would be happier if they could earn only a little more each week. Do you find yourself periodically siding with this majority, falling into the "if only" trap.

"If only I had a new car, I would be satisfied. If only I lived in that nice house, I would be content. If only I had a particular job, I would be happy." The list is endless.

The Bible offers a sharp contrast to this attitude. As someone has said,

Money will buy:

A bed but not sleep;

Books but not brains;

Food but not an appetite;

A house but not a home;

Medicine but not health;

Amusement but not happiness;

A crucifix but not a Savior.

IS MONEY EVIL?

Money is not evil. It is morally neutral. Money can be used for good, such as supporting missionaries or building hospitals. It also can be used for evil, such as financing illegal drugs and pornography.

Examine 1 Timothy 6:10 carefully: "For the love of money is the root of all evils." The Bible does not condemn money itself, only the misuse of or a wrong attitude toward money. Moreover, particularly in the Old Testament, many of the godliest people were among the wealthiest people of the day. Job, Abraham and David were all wealthy, and yet they did not allow it to interfere with their relationship with the Lord.

Nevertheless, Scripture warns that riches can destroy a spiritually fruitful life. "The seed sown among thorns is the one who hears the word, but then worldly anxiety and the lure of riches choke the word and it bears no fruit" (Matthew 13:22).

Also, it is easy for those who have resources to turn away from God. "I will take them into this rich and fertile land, as I promised their ancestors. There they will have all the food they want, and they will live comfortably. But they will turn away and worship other gods. They will reject me and break my covenant." (Deuteronomy 31:20, GNT). Someone once observed, "For every 99 people who can be poor and remain close to Christ, only one can become wealthy and maintain a close relationship with him." It must be human nature to cling to the Lord when it's obvious that only he can provide our needs. Once people become prosperous, they often take the Lord for granted because they no longer think they have as much need of him.

WILL GODLY PEOPLE ALWAYS
PROSPER FINANCIALLY?

Some Christians embrace one of two extremes. Some say if you are really spiritual, you must be poor because wealth and a close relationship with Christ cannot coexist. The second and opposite extreme is the belief that if a Christian has faith, he or she will enjoy uninterrupted financial prosperity.

One end of the spectrum teaches that godliness can occur only in an environment of poverty. However, we already have noted that money is morally neutral and can be used for good or evil. In the Old Testament the Lord extended the reward of abundance to the children of Israel when they were obedient, while the threat of poverty was one of the consequences of disobedience. Deuteronomy 30:15-16, RSVCE reads, "See, I have today set before you life and good, death and evil. If you obey the commandments of the LORD, your God, which I am giving you today, loving the LORD, your God, and walking in his ways, and keeping his commandments, statutes and ordinances, you will live and grow numerous, and the LORD, your God, will bless you in the land you are entering to possess."

Moreover, Psalm 35:27 (GNT) reads, "He is pleased with the success of his servant." "Beloved, I hope that you are prospering in every respect and are in good health, just as your soul is prospering" (3 John 1:2). Let me emphasize that again. The Bible does not say that a godly person must live in poverty. A godly person may have material resources.

There are those on the other hand who believe all Christians who truly have faith always will prosper. This extreme also is in error.

Study the life of Joseph. He is the classic example of a faithful person who experienced both prosperity and poverty. He was born into a prosperous family, then was thrown into a pit and sold into slavery by his jealous brothers. He became a household slave in a wealthy Egyptian's home. His master, Potiphar, promoted Joseph to head the household. Later Joseph made the righteous decision not to commit adultery with Potiphar's wife. Because of that decision, however, he was thrown into prison for years. In God's timing, Joseph ultimately was elevated to the position of prime minister of Egypt.

> *If you love money, you will never be satisfied; if you long to be rich, you will never get all you want. It is useless.*
>
> Ecclesiastes 5:10, GNT

Let's examine three reasons why the godly may not prosper.

148

1. Violating a Scriptural Principle.

You may be giving generously but acting dishonestly. You may be honest but not properly fulfilling your work responsibilities. You may be a faithful employee but head-over-heels in debt. You may be completely out of debt but not giving.

One of the biggest benefits of this book is that we explore what the entire Bible teaches about money. Those who do not understand all the requirements may neglect critical areas of responsibility and suffer financially.

2. Building of Godly Character.

An example of the Lord developing character in a people before prospering them is found in Deuteronomy 8:16-18:

> [He] . . . fed you in the wilderness with manna, a food unknown to your ancestors, that he might afflict you and test you, but also make you prosperous in the end. Otherwise, you might say in your heart, "It is my own power and the strength of my own hand that has got me this wealth." Remember then the LORD, your God, for he is the one who gives you the power to get wealth, by fulfilling, as he has now done, the covenant he swore to your ancestors.

The Lord knew the children of Israel had to be humble before they could handle wealth. Our Father knows us better than we know ourselves. In his infinite wisdom he knows exactly how much he can entrust to us at any time without harming our relationship with him.

3. The Mystery of God's Sovereignty.

Hebrews 11:1-35 lists people who triumphed miraculously by exercising their faith in the living God. But in verse 36 the writer directs our attention abruptly to godly people who lived by faith and gained God's approval, yet experienced poverty. The Lord ultimately chooses how much to entrust to each person. And sometimes we simply can't understand or explain his decisions.

Let's summarize: The Scriptures teach neither the necessity of poverty nor uninterrupted prosperity. What the Bible teaches is the responsibility of being a faithful steward. Please review the diagram on the next page and the contrasts between the three perspectives.

	Poverty	Stewardship	Prosperity
Possessions are	Evil	A responsibility	A right
I work to	Meet only basic needs	Serve Christ	Become rich
Godly people are	Poor	Faithful	Wealthy
Ungodly people are	Wealthy	Unfaithful	Poor
I give	Because I must	Because I love God	To get
My spending is	Without gratitude to God	Prayerful and responsible	Carefree and consumptive

THE LORD'S PERSPECTIVE OF PROSPERITY

Before we leave the issue of prosperity, it is important to understand that the Lord's perspective of prosperity is contrary to that of our culture. The Lord evaluates true riches based on his spiritual value system. This contrast is stated most clearly in the book of Revelation. The godly poor are rich in God's sight. "I [the Lord] know your tribulation and poverty, but you are rich" (Revelation 2:9). Those who are wealthy yet do not enjoy a close relationship with Christ are actually poor. "For you say, 'I am rich and affluent and have no need of anything,' and yet do not realize that you are wretched, pitiable, poor, blind, and naked" (Revelation 3:17). True prosperity extends far beyond material possessions. True prosperity is gauged by how well we know Jesus Christ and by how closely we follow him.

INSTRUCTIONS TO THOSE WHO ARE PROSPEROUS

Are you rich? Sometimes we feel rich and sometimes we don't. It usually depends on who we are around. Most of us define a rich person as a person who has more money than we do. But if we compare our living standards to all the people who have lived throughout history or even with the rest of the billions of people living on the earth today, the majority of us who live in this nation are rich.

The Lord knew the rich would face serious spiritual danger. So Scripture offers three instructions for those who are rich in this world.

1. Do not be proud.

"Tell the rich in this present age not to be proud" (1 Timothy 6:17). Wealth tends to produce pride. For several years, Howard drove two vehicles. The first was an old pickup truck that cost $100. It looked as if it cost $100! When he drove that truck to the bank drive-in-window to cash a check, he was humble. He knew the cashier was going to double-check his account to make certain that the driver of that truck had sufficient funds to cover the withdrawal. Howard waited patiently while she checked. When he received the money, he was so grateful. He drove away with a song in his heart and praises on his lips.

Howard's other vehicle was a well-preserved, secondhand automobile that was expensive when it was new. When he drove that car to the bank, he appeared to be a different person. He deserved a certain amount of respect. He was not quite as patient when the cashier examined my account, and when he received the money, he was not as grateful. Wealth stimulates conceit.

James 1:9-10 addresses this issue: "The brother in lowly circumstances should take pride in his high standing and the rich one in his lowliness, for he will pass away, 'like the flower of the field.'" The poor should be encouraged as children of the King of kings, while the rich are to remain humble because life is short. If you are rich, you need the constant reminder to be humble before the Lord and other people.

2. Put no confidence in your assets.

"Tell the rich in the present age not to be proud and not to rely on so uncertain a thing as wealth but rather on God, who richly provides us with all things for our enjoyment" (1 Timothy 6:17). This can create a tremendous inner struggle. It's easy for us to trust in the tangible assets we have accumulated. We know that money can buy goods and services. It has so much power that it is easy to be fooled into thinking that money supplies our needs and offers security. Money can become our first love. We tend to trust in the seen rather than in the invisible living God. This is why we need to constantly remind ourselves to walk by faith rather than by sight.

3. Give generously.

"Tell them to do good, to be rich in good works, to be generous, ready to share, thus accumulating as treasure a good foundation for the future, so as to win the life that is true life" (1 Timothy 6:18-19).

"The Gospels are full of examples of God's favor being focused on the poor, not the rich. Jesus enters the world in a stable and lives in a working-class family. St. Joseph was a laborer, not a worker with fine wood. Through the years there have been many who have preached the gospel of the full stomach. But it is not the gospel of Jesus. Most of the saints who were born into wealth renounced it sooner or later" (Fr. Vincent Serpa O.P., www.catholic.com/quickquestions/does-god-want-us-to-be-wealthy, Catholic Answers).

One of the most effective antidotes for the potential disease of loving money is "setting the finish line." Determine a maximum amount that you will accumulate. After you have reached your goal, give the rest to build God's kingdom.

CONTRAST

Society says: Wealth brings happiness and security, and I can use it for my own comfort any way I choose.

Scripture says: True joy is based on my relationship with Christ. In him alone will I trust. If I am prosperous, I should be generous and ready to share.

COMMITMENT

I will consistently study the Bible to maintain God's perspective of money and possessions.

SEVENTEEN

CRISIS

The Storms of Life

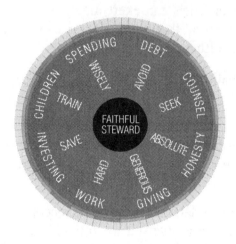

There was a knock at the door, and Howard and Bev glanced at each other. Would he be all they had dreamed?

They raced for the door, threw it open, and there he was. Tiny, gorgeous, and absolutely precious. Four-day-old Andrew, the baby they hoped to adopt, captured their hearts the moment they held him in their arms.

Several months later they began to suspect that Andrew might have some physical challenges. Tragically, his birth mother had been addicted to powerful narcotics during her pregnancy, and the doctors discovered he had been born with only a fraction of his brain. It was a very difficult time for Howard and Bev—emotionally, physically, and financially. Andrew required multiple surgeries. Because he suffered constant pain, he required around-the-clock care, which led to Bev's exhaustion and almost a complete physical breakdown.

Some challenges build slowly and can be anticipated; others appear without warning. Some are resolved quickly; others are chronic. Some reflect the consequences of our actions; others are completely beyond our control. Some crises impact an entire nation; others are isolated to us as individuals.

A job loss, major illness, birth of a special-needs child, business reversal, death of a family member, identity theft, military deployment of a breadwinner, home foreclosure, bankruptcy, or worldwide financial crisis can exert major pressure on us and our finances. Surveys reveal that many marriages simply don't survive the stress of these difficulties.

We call these challenges the "storms of life." While some of the storms amount to little more than a blustery rain shower, others feel like a category-five hurricane.

> **Please remember this one thing:** No matter what the crisis, you don't face it alone. Jesus Christ is with you every step of the way.

Put yourself in the sandals of a few of God's people in the Bible who faced terrifying category-five storms. Job—in a matter of just a few hours—lost his children, his financial resources, and ultimately his health. Joseph was sold into slavery and thrown into prison. Moses and the children of Israel faced annihilation by Egypt's powerful army at the Red Sea. Daniel was tossed into the lion's den. Paul was beaten, stoned, and left for dead on his missionary journeys. The list goes on and on.

Although storms are often emotional, scary, and painful, if we maintain God's perspective, we can survive and even grow through such dark days (and nights!).

GOD'S ROLE

When facing a crisis, nothing is more important than knowing who

God is—his love, care, control, and power. Only the Bible reveals the true extent of God's involvement in our challenges. If we have an inadequate or warped view of God and his purposes, then we won't fully embrace and learn from our challenges. What's more, we will forfeit the peace, contentment, and even joy that God makes available to us in the midst of the storm.

God Loves You

First John 4:8 (GNT) sums up God's very nature: "Whoever does not love does not know God, for God is love." God loves you, and throughout your whole life remains intimately involved with you as an individual. Psalm 139:17-18 reveals, "How precious to me are your designs, O God; How vast the sum of them! Were I to count them, they would outnumber the sand . . . ." In other words, the Creator of the universe is always thinking about you!

When you think about it, John 15:9 has to be one of the most encouraging verses in all of the Bible. Jesus says, "As the Father has loved me, so also I love you." Don't skim over those words! Let the implications sink in for a moment. Consider how much God the Father loves God the Son. They have existed forever in the closest possible relationship with a deep, unfathomable love for each other. And Jesus says this is how much he loves you!

In any crisis, it's critical to be reminded of God's unfailing love and faithfulness. Why? Because it's so very easy to become discouraged and even lose hope in such times. It's easy to forget God's love and care for you, especially when adversity first strikes—or goes on and on for what feels like an eternity.

Jeremiah the prophet was completely discouraged. He wrote: "The thought of my homeless poverty is wormwood and gall; remembering it over and over leaves my soul downcast within me" (Lamentations 3:19-20). But then he remembered the Lord, "But I will call this to mind, as my reason to have hope. The favors of the LORD are not exhausted, his mercies are not spent; they are renewed each morning, so great is your faithfulness" (Lamentations 3:21-23).

It is helpful to meditate on passages such as these: "Keep your lives free from the love of money, and be satisfied with what you have. For God has said, 'I will never leave you; I will never abandon you.' Let us be bold, then, and say, 'The Lord is my helper, I will not be afraid. What can anyone do to me?'" (Hebrews 13:5-6, GNT). "Who, then, can separate us from the love of Christ? Can trouble do it, or hardship or persecution or hunger or poverty or danger or death? No, in all these things we have complete victory through him who loved us!" (Romans 8:35, 37, GNT).

I've discovered that even in a crisis, the Lord will do kind things that offer clear evidence of his love and care for us. Consider Joseph. While a slave, "[Joseph's master] saw that the Lord was with Joseph and had made him successful in everything he did . . . " (Genesis 39:3, GNT), so his master put him in charge of all he owned. Later in prison, "the Lord was with Joseph and blessed him, so that the jailer was pleased with him . . . " (Genesis 39:21, GNT).

God Has Sovereign Control

As we studied earlier, God, through his sovereignty, is ultimately in control of every event. This is but a sampling of passages that affirm his control: "Our God is in heaven; he does whatever he wishes" (Psalm 115:3, GNT). "Yours, O LORD, is the sovereignty; you are exalted as head over all" (1 Chronicles 29:11). "Whatever the LORD wishes, he does, in heaven and in earth" (Psalm 135:6). "I [the LORD] said that my plans would never fail that I would do everything I intended to do" (Isaiah 46:10, GNT). "For there is nothing that God cannot do" (Luke 1:37, GNT).

Even of difficult events the Lord's sovereignty rules. "I am the LORD, and there is no other, I form the light and create the darkness, I make well-being and create woe; I, the LORD who does all these" (Isaiah 45:6-7).

God Has a Purpose for Adversity

The Cecropia moth emerges from its cocoon only after a long, exhausting struggle to free itself. A young boy, wishing to help the moth, carefully slit the exterior of the cocoon. Soon it came out, but its wings were shriveled, and couldn't function. What the young boy didn't realize was that the moth's struggle to liberate itself from the cocoon was essential to develop its wings—and its ability to fly.

Much like the cocoon of the Cecropia moth, adversity has a part to play in our lives as well. God uses those difficult, sometimes heartbreaking times to mature us in Christ. James 1:2-4 (GNT) says it this way: "My friends, consider yourselves fortunate when all kinds of trials come your way, for you know that when your faith succeeds in facing such trials the result is the ability to endure. Make sure that your endurance carries you all the way without failing, so that you may be perfect and complete, lacking nothing."

Many times, challenging circumstances can work for our ultimate benefit. Romans 8:28-29 (GNT) tells us, "We know that in all things God works for the good of those who love him, those whom he has called according to his purpose. Those whom God had already chosen he also set apart to become like his Son, so that the Son would be the first among many believers." And the primary good that God works in our lives is to make us more like Christ.

We see this same thought expressed in Hebrews 12:5-6, 10-11,

> My son, do not disdain the discipline of the Lord or lose heart when reproved by him; for whom the Lord loves, he disciplines; he scourges every son he acknowledges . . . . They [our earthly fathers] disciplined us for a short time as seemed right to them, but he [the Lord] does so for our benefit, in order that we may share his holiness. At the time, all discipline seems a cause not for joy but for pain, yet later it brings the peaceful fruit of righteousness to those who are trained by it.

God makes no mistakes. He knows exactly what he wants us to become, and also knows exactly what is necessary to produce that result in our lives.

The Catechism teaches, "The Father who gives us life cannot not but give us the nourishment life requires—all appropriate goods and blessings, both material and spiritual."

To those who seek the kingdom of God and his righteousness, he has promised to give all else besides. Since everything indeed belongs to God, he who possesses God wants for nothing, if he himself is not found wanting before God. (St. Cyprian, *De Dom. orat.* 21:PL 4, 534A.) (CCC 2830).

Howard and Bev have endured—and benefited from—many storms. The one surrounding Andrew's birth with most of his brain missing until his death 11 years later drew them much closer to each other and to the Lord. Through the crucible of their pain and tears, many of the Bible's truths grew from wispy theory into rock-solid reality. They began to grasp how deeply God loved and cared for Andrew; and for them. Although they would never want to repeat this experience, they are incredibly grateful for how the Lord used it in their lives.

Often, in difficult circumstances, our only choice is to turn to God. St. Augustine writes, "When I am completely united to you there will be no more sorrow or trials: entirely full of you, my life will be complete."

Please don't miss this point. You and I need to recognize difficulties as opportunities to grow into the people God wants us to be. In adversity we learn things we just couldn't learn any other way.

We know what you're thinking . . . "That's easy for you to say. You have no idea what we've been through." Granted. But then, we could also say, "You have no idea what we have been through during our 45 years of marriage." And yet the Lord Jesus has stood with us in every crisis, every heartache, every difficult decision. Every one of those incidents, painful as they were, brought us closer to him and closer to each other.

You can be comforted knowing that your loving heavenly Father is in absolute control of every situation you will ever face. He intends to use each circumstance for a good purpose. First Thessalonians 5:18 says it well, "Give thanks in all circumstances, for this is God's will for you in Christ Jesus."

TRUSTING GOD

We should view crises through the lens of God's love, faithfulness and control.

When Bev reached the point of total exhaustion in serving baby Andrew, Howard and Bev knew it would be physically impossible for them to care for him on our own. Desperately needing to rest and recover, they decided to admit him for a time to a facility that specialized in caring for profoundly handicapped children.

This was a deeply emotional time, and they openly wept in the admittance room. Then Howard looked up and noticed a painting of Jesus hanging on the wall. When he looked at the picture, it helped him reflect on God's faithfulness, and he experienced peace. When Howard looked away and thought only of the circumstances, his tears flowed. In that moment, he experienced the reality of Isaiah 26:3 (GNT): "You, LORD, give perfect peace to those who keep their purpose firm and put their trust in you."

The Bible makes it clear that God offers security only in himself—not in money, not in possessions, not in a career, and not in other people. External things offer the illusion of security, but the Lord alone can be fully trusted. "The LORD is good; he protect his people in times of trouble; he takes care of those who turn to him" (Nahum 1:7, GNT). "My foes treat me harshly all the day; yes, many are my attackers. O Most High, when I am afraid, in you I place my trust" (Psalm 56:3-4).

THE EYE OF THE STORM

There are several things we can do to survive—and even grow—when we find ourselves in the storm.

Get your financial house in order

We've been close to many people facing gut-wrenching financial storms. And the first question they usually ask is: How can I solve the problem?

Jesus answers the question this way in Matthew 7:24-25 (GNT): ". . . Anyone who hears these words of mine **and obeys them** is like a wise man who built his house on the rock. The rain poured down, the rivers flooded over, and the wind blew hard against that house. But it did not fall, because it was built on rock" (emphasis added).

The key to solving your financial problems is learning and applying God's way of handling money. It truly is that simple. That's why this book is so important. When you finish it, you will know God's framework for managing money. But knowing is only half of what you need. The other half is applying what you have learned. It may take a long time and a lot of effort to navigate the storm, but you will know the basics of what you should do.

Part of what you've learned is to be a generous giver. When facing a financial crisis the tendency is to hold on tightly to what we have, and become less generous. A key passage in the book of Acts, however, shows us a different way. In Acts 11:28-29 (GNT) we read: "One of them, named Agabus [a prophet] stood up and by the power of the Spirit predicted that a severe famine was about to come over all the earth. (It came when Claudius was emperor.) The disciples decided that they each would send as much as they could to help their fellow believers who lived in Judea."

Think about this. The Holy Spirit revealed through a prophet that a severe famine was coming soon, and their first reaction was to give! Don't allow a crisis or a pending crisis to stop you from remaining generous. You may not be able to give as much as you did previously, but still give.

It's also important to quickly evaluate how the circumstance will impact your finances, and to make the necessary adjustments for any diminished income or increased expenses. And don't forget to communicate! Tell the Lord, and if you are married, tell each other your feelings and concerns. How important is this? It's important enough to schedule a time every day to share, so you can encourage each other. Evelyn and I discovered that a crisis doesn't have to damage a marriage; in fact, it can be a catalyst to improve it. We are fully persuaded that God intends married couples to grow closer together during a crisis rather than allowing the difficulties to damage their marriage.

Never go through a storm alone

Without repeating the advice in the "Counsel" chapter, I want to emphasize the importance of not going it alone. It is almost impossible to make the wisest decisions in isolation when experiencing a crisis.

Seek advice from people who have been through similar situations. You will draw strength not only from their emotional support, but also from their experience. There are people all around you who have weathered serious life storms, and you can gain from their knowledge, learning mistakes to avoid and resources to help. Ask your church and friends to pray; it's their most powerful contribution.

Live one day at a time

Robert Johnson built an extraordinarily successful construction business from scratch. He was extremely generous and enjoyed a wonderful reputation. Then came the crushing financial crisis of 2008 — crippling his business and pushing him to the brink of bankruptcy.

Confiding in me one day, Robert said, "In a crisis, the tendency is to look ahead and become overwhelmed with all the problems. We are to plan ahead, but for our mental and emotional health we must follow what Jesus Christ told us: "So do not worry about tomorrow; it will have enough worries of its own. There is no need to add to the troubles each day brings" (Matthew 6:34, GNT).

Live focused on today! And if the crisis becomes severe, focus on one moment at a time in close relationship with Christ. This is not "escape from reality," but rather; it is a practical way to stay close to the only one who can help us through the challenge.

Be patient, waiting for God's timing

Expectations can be damaging during a crisis. When we assume that the Lord will solve our problems in a certain way by a certain time, we set ourselves up for disappointment and frustration.

Someone described patience as accepting a difficult situation without giving God a deadline for removing it. Remember, God's primary purpose in allowing a crisis in the first place is to conform you to Jesus Christ. He is at work in your life, and knows exactly how long it will take to produce the results he wants. Ecclesiastes 3:1 says, "There is an appointed time for everything, and a time for every affair under the heavens."

The late Larry Burkett used to say with a smile, "God is seldom early, but he's never late." Be patient. Be careful not to set deadlines for the Lord to act.

Work diligently to solve your problems, with the recognition that you need the moment by moment help and counsel of the Lord who loves you. Philippians 4:6-7 is one of Howard's favorite Bible passages when facing difficulties. Every phrase is loaded with meaning. "Have no anxiety at all, but in everything, by prayer and petition, with thanksgiving, make your requests known to God. Then the peace of God that surpasses all understanding will guard your hearts and minds in Christ Jesus."

Forgive others

Imagine you are a teenager, deeply loved by your father. Your siblings sell you into slavery, and for the next 13 years you are a slave and a prisoner. Amazingly, on one unbelievable day, you find yourself elevated to second in command of the world's most powerful nation. Several years later, your starving siblings—the ones who betrayed you—beg you for food. What's your response: retaliation or forgiveness?

This is the question Joseph had to answer, and he forgave. How was he able to do this? Because he recognized that God had orchestrated his circumstances—even the ones that were so deeply traumatic and painful. "God sent me ahead of you to rescue you in this amazing way and to make sure that you and your descendants survive. So it was not really you who sent me here, but God . . . " (Genesis 45:7-8, GNT).

God realizes how critical it is for us to forgive those who are involved in causing our crisis, regardless of their motivation. One of the most impressive characteristics of Jesus Christ was his willingness to forgive. Imagine hanging on a cross in excruciating agony, and at the same time praying for those who had crucified you: "Forgive them Father! They don't know what they are doing" (Luke 23:34, GNT).

When the apostle Peter asked Jesus if he should forgive someone seven times, he responded, "not seven times . . . but seventy times seven" (Matthew 18:22, GNT). He then told a parable about a servant who was forgiven a large debt by his master but refused to forgive a fellow servant a small debt. Christ describes what happens to the unforgiving servant: "The king was very angry, and he sent the servant to jail to be punished until he should pay back the whole amount . . . that is how my Father in heaven will treat everyone of you unless you forgive your brother from your heart" (Matthew 18:34-35, GNT).

In order to grow more like Christ and experience the benefits he intends for us during a crisis, we must forgive. And more than forgive, we are to be kind, compassionate, and seek to be a blessing. "Be kind and tender-hearted to one another, and forgive one another, as God has forgiven you through Christ" (Ephesians 4:32, GNT). "Do not pay back evil with evil or cursing with cursing instead, pay back with a blessing, because a blessing is what God promised to give you when he called you" (1 Peter 3:9, GNT).

Lack of forgiveness can be a daily battle, particularly if the crisis has been horribly hurtful. But it harms the person who refuses to forgive. Howard's wife Bev describes it as swallowing poison and hoping the other person will die. When we refuse to forgive, the bitterness in our heart can turn toxic, consuming our thoughts and eating away our emotional health. Forgiveness and seeking to bless the other person, however, leads to freedom.

It is imperative to pray regularly for the Lord to give us the desire to forgive, and then to give us his love for the people who may have harmed us. Jesus tells us also to pray for them, "But now I tell you:

love your enemies and pray for those who persecute you" (Matthew 5:44, GNT). It's hard to remain bitter toward someone for whom you are praying regularly.

COMMON CHALLENGES

Let's examine two of the most common financial challenges people face.

Job loss

Losing your job ranks among life's most stressful events—not just for you but for your spouse as well if you are married. Meet together as soon as possible after the job loss, and discuss ways to minimize the emotional and financial toll on both of you. And encourage each other because often a job loss is a blessing in disguise. God may bring you a better career opportunity, and it can build your faith as you experience him providing your needs even without a job.

Next, formulate a game plan for the job search—from drafting a resume to networking with friends. When you lose a job, your full-time job should be finding a new job.

In addition to cutting back on spending for discretionary items, there are two financial goals to keep in mind. First, make every effort to avoid using debt for living expenses. Many people mask the real situation by using debt to fund current spending. Make good, hard decisions not to spend one penny you don't have to. Every borrowed penny must be repaid with interest, and although spending it is easy, repayment is always hard work.

Second, do what you can to maintain health insurance. You may be able to assume your health insurance coverage through a plan from your former employer. If not, get advice from others on cost-efficient coverage.

Illness or accident

If you suffer a major illness or accident, it's a double whammy. Medical expenses pile on as income plunges. If the condition is severe enough to prevent future employment, you will need to make permanent adjustments. And if either health insurance or disability coverage is inadequate, it can be financially catastrophic.

If married, be prepared for the possibility that one of you may need to make important decisions without the benefit of input from the other. Evelyn and I have decided that if one of us is seriously ill, the other will make the financial and health-related decisions. We are each familiar with the location of all important records and know how to use them.

Don't be embarrassed to make your needs known to your family, friends, and church. Extend to them the opportunity to help meet your needs. Giving to those in need is a big part of what it means to follow Christ. Galatians 6:2 (GNT) reminds us, "Help carry one another's burdens, and in this way you will obey the law of Christ."

PREPARING FOR FUTURE STORMS

You can't prevent every difficulty, but you can prepare to survive them by building a solid relationship with the Lord—and your spouse, if you are married—and by improving your finances. The healthier your finances, the better you will be able to cope. Proverbs 27:12 (GNT) says, "Sensible people will see trouble coming and avoid it, but an unthinking person will walk right into it and regret it later."

The more time you spend getting to know God and what he reveals in the Bible—and applying what you've learned—the better prepared you will be to weather life's storms.

One of the biggest benefits of making progress on your journey to true financial freedom is that it provides a financial margin when you find yourself facing an unexpected crisis. By the time Andrew was born, Howard and Bev had paid off all their debts including the mortgage. Even though they were debt-free at the time, they knew that his medical expenses would be a challenge. And they were. Their freedom from debt, however, helped them to focus on Andrew and each other, as they dealt with his problems.

CONTRAST

Society says: If I have a crisis the Government should come to my rescue.

Scripture says: A close relationship with God is our strength in a time of crisis.

COMMITMENT

I will analyze my spending and the everyday budget that I have created and will create a crisis budget so that I am prepared for a crisis situation.

EIGHTEEN

SUMMING IT ALL UP

At the beginning of this book we asked why the Bible says so much about money—more than 2,500 verses. The Lord knew that how we handled money would help determine the intimacy of our relationship with him. The Lord also wanted to provide us with a blueprint for handling money so that we could be faithful in this practical area of life.

The fundamental truth for us to understand is that God has retained the responsibilities of ownership of possessions, sovereign control of events and provision of needs. As people, we are not designed to shoulder these responsibilities. However, the Lord delegated certain important tasks to us as stewards.

169

Review the wheel diagram on the previous page and the eight areas of our responsibility.

FINANCIAL FAITHFULNESS IS A JOURNEY—DO NOT BECOME DISCOURAGED

Applying God's financial principles is a journey that takes time. It's easy to become discouraged. When you finish this book, your finances may not be completely under control. Don't get frustrated. It takes the average person at least a year to apply most of these principles. Again, I want to encourage you to enroll in a Compass Catholic small group study. It is an excellent way to receive encouragement and help in implementing these principles.

FAITHFULNESS IN SMALL MATTERS IS IMPORTANT

Because of a lack of resources, many people become frustrated by their inability to solve their financial problems. Remember; simply be faithful with what you have—whether it is little or much.

Some give up too soon. They abandon the goal of becoming debt free. They stop trying to increase their saving or giving. For them the task seems impossible. And it may be impossible without the Lord's help. Your job is to make a genuine effort, no matter how small it may appear. Then leave the results to God. Don't be discouraged. Be diligent. Be persistent. Be faithful in even the smallest matters.

A good friend once asked me what was the most valuable lesson I had learned from the Compass small group studies. I've had time to reflect on that question for some time now. I think the most valuable lesson has been the realization that I needed to consistently review Scripture. I noticed this in preparation for a class. If I had invested little time studying the Bible during the previous weeks, I would discover that I had been molded ever so subtly by the views of our culture. Romans 12:2, (RSV CE) presents this problem and the solution: "And do not be conformed to this world, but be transformed by the renewing of your mind." The only way for any of us to renew our minds (to discover and preserve the correct perspective) is to expose ourselves to Scripture regularly.

The Bible has the answers to the financial problems of the sophisticated twenty-first century. The eternal principles of Scripture are practical in any culture and in any century.

CONTENTMENT

At the beginning of this book we said that one of our objectives was that you would learn to be content. In 1 Timothy 6:8, Paul issues this challenging statement: "if we have food and clothing, we shall be content with that." Study this passage carefully. It declares that if you have food and clothing (clothes and shelter), you should be content. Our culture has restated this verse to read something like this: "If you can afford the finest food to eat, wear the latest fashions, drive the newest luxury automobile and live in a beautiful home in the nicest section of town, then you can be happy." Nothing could be further from the truth.

As Christian stewards, we receive God's gifts gratefully, cultivate them responsibly, share them lovingly in justice with others, and return them with increase to the Lord (*Stewardship: A Disciple's Response,* USCCB, Appendix 1).

There are three elements in learning to be content:

Know what God requires of a steward.

Fulfill those requirements faithfully.

Trust God to do his part.

Once we understand God's responsibilities and we have been faithful in fulfilling our responsibilities as stewards, we can be content. Our loving heavenly Father will entrust us with the possessions he knows will be best for us at any particular time — whether much or little.

Biblical contentment is not to be equated with laziness, complacency, social insensitivity or apathy. Because we serve the living and dynamic God, Christians should always be improving. Contentment does not exclude properly motivated ambition. We already have discovered that God wants us to work hard. I believe we should have a burning desire to be faithful stewards of the talents and possessions he has entrusted to us. Biblical contentment is an inner peace that accepts what God has chosen for our present vocation, station in life and financial state. Hebrews 13:5 emphasizes this: "Let your life be free from love of money but be content with what you have, for he has said, 'I will never forsake you or abandon you.'"

NOW IS THE TIME!

As Howard mentioned earlier, God revealed to him that America will experience some very, very difficult financial times during his lifetime, and we don't believe that we have seen the worst, even with all that has happened recently.

You now know the biblical framework for managing money. We plead with you to seize this opportunity! Become diligent in your efforts to get out of debt, give generously, budget persistently and work as unto the Lord. In short, become a faithful steward by getting your finances in order God's way.

It is clear that the economic storm is going to burst against this nation's financial house. If you have built your house on the rock-solid principles found in the Bible, not only will you survive financially, but you will be in a position to help others less fortunate.

We appreciate the effort you have invested in reading this book. We pray this has given you a greater appreciation for the Bible, helped you become financially healthy, and above all else, nurtured your love for Jesus Christ. May the Lord richly bless you in every way as you draw close to him.

QUESTIONS AND ANSWERS

This section deals with some frequently asked and sometimes controversial questions. When Scripture does not specifically answer the question, my opinion is given to stir your thinking.

Question: What is God's perspective on paying taxes?

Answer: That's the same question that was asked of Jesus: "Is it against our Law for us to pay taxes to the Roman emperor, or not? But Jesus saw through their trick and said to them, 'Show me a silver coin. Whose face and name are these on it?' 'The emperors,' they answered. So Jesus said, 'Well, then, pay to the emperor what belongs to the emperor and pay to God what belongs to God'" (Luke 20:22-25, GNT).

This a clear example of the contrast between the practices of our society and the teachings of Scripture. Avoid paying taxes at any cost, most people rationalize. After all, the government squanders much of the money it receives.

A very fine line often exists between tax avoidance and tax evasion, and many experience a strong temptation to misappropriate funds that are legally owed to the government. An estimated $100 billion a year in taxes is lost through tax evasion.

I am not condoning the waste and excesses found in government. In fact, I believe a citizen should try to influence government to be more efficient and responsive. However, the Bible tells us of an additional responsibility: pay your taxes! "Everyone must obey state authorities, because no authority exists without God's permission, and the existing authorities have been put there by God. That is also why you pay taxes, because the authorities are working for God when they fulfill their duties. Pay, then, what you owe them . . . " (Romans 13:1, 6-7, GNT).

Question: How does the Bible define financial success?

Answer: According to Scripture, financial success is achieved by being a faithful steward. This is not the standard used by most people to judge success. Usually, the more wealth a person has accumulated, the more he or she is considered to have succeeded. However, according to the Bible it is impossible to tell if a person is truly "successful" by looking at his or her external circumstances, possessions or position. If we had seen Joseph or Paul in prison, Daniel in the lion's den or Job in his affliction, how many of us would have considered them successful?

Webster's definition of success is "the degree or measure of attaining a desired end." According to Scripture the desired end for us is to become faithful stewards. After we have fulfilled our responsibility by becoming faithful stewards, it is up to God to decide whether or not to entrust us with wealth.

Question: Is it permissible for a Christian to be ambitious?

Answer: Scripture does not condemn ambition. Paul was ambitious. "Therefore we aspire to please him . . . For we must all appear before the judgment seat of Christ, so that each one may receive recompense, according to what he did in the body, whether good or evil" (2 Corinthians 5:9-10).

What is strongly denounced is selfish ambition. "But if you have . . . selfish ambition in your heart, do not boast and be false to the truth. Wisdom of this kind does not come down from above, but is earthly, unspiritual, demonic. For where jealousy and selfish ambition exists, there is disorder and every foul practice" (James 3:14-16).

The Bible is not the enemy of ambition, only of a wrong type of ambition. Our ambition should not be motivated out of an egotistical desire. "And you, do you seek great things for yourself? Do not seek them!" (Jeremiah 45:5). Our ambition should be to please Christ. We should have a burning desire to become increasingly faithful stewards in using the possessions and skills entrusted to us.

Question: Should wives work in a job outside the home?

Answer: For many reasons, women are involved in jobs of all kinds. Married women work to provide additional income for their families, to express their creativity or to enjoy the work environment. Widows and divorcees often must work to provide for their needs. A Stanford University study shows that wives who work outside the home carry a particularly heavy load of responsibility. With their job and their household activities, these wives work 70 to 80 hours a week.

In our opinion, during children's early formative years it is preferable for a mother to be home whenever the children are home. Titus 2:4-5 reads, ". . . train younger women to love their husbands and children, to be self-controlled, chaste, good homemakers." It is ideal for a mother of young children to limit working outside the home to those times when the children are not at home unless family finances depend upon her income. As children mature, the wife will have increased freedom to pursue work outside the home. Proverbs 31:10-27 reads:

> When one finds a worthy wife . . . She brings him good, and not evil, all the days of her life. She obtains wool and flax and makes cloth with skillful hands. Like merchant ships, she secures her provisions from afar. She rises while it is still night, and distributes food to her household . . . She picks out a field to purchase; out of her earnings she plants a vineyard . . . She puts her hands to the distaff, and her fingers ply the spindle. She reaches out her hands to the poor . . . She makes her own coverlets; fine linen and purple are her clothing. Her husband is prominent at the city gates as he sits with the elders of the land. She makes garments and sells them, and stocks the merchants with belts . . . She watches the conduct of her household, and eats not her food in idleness.

Proverbs 31 paints a beautiful picture of the working wife living a balanced life with the thrust of her activity toward the home. Our opinion is that a wife's work is not so much in the home as it is for the home. The Bible does not say that a wife should be confined to four walls, but rather it describes a woman involved in activities that relate to the home.

Some women are gifted as homemakers. However, other women have the aptitude and desire to work outside the home. Whether or not a wife works outside a home is a decision that the husband and wife should make prayerfully and with full agreement.

If a wife works to produce more income for a family, it is important to analyze exactly how much income, after taxes and expenses, her work contributes to the family. Couples often are surprised to learn that this income is not as much as they had expected.

Question: What does the Bible tell us about partnerships?

Answer: In 2 Corinthians 6:14-17, we read,

> Do not be yoked with those who are different, with unbelievers. For what partnership do righteousness and lawlessness have? Or what fellowship does light have with darkness? . . . Or what has a believer in common with an unbeliever? . . . Therefore, come forth from them and be separate,' says the Lord.

Scripture clearly discourages business partnerships with those who do not know Christ. Many have violated this principle and have suffered financially.

In our opinion we also should be very careful before entering into a partnership with another Christian. Howard would consider only a few people as potential partners. He has known these individuals for years and has observed their commitment to the Lord. He knows their strengths and weaknesses and has seen them consistently handle money faithfully. Do not rush into a partnership! Prayerfully evaluate what it may entail.

Before forming a partnership, reduce your understandings and agreements into written form with your future partner. In this written document provide a method to dissolve the partnership if necessary.

If you are not able to agree in writing, do not become partners.

Question: Why do the wicked prosper?

Answer: This is a disturbing question God's people have asked for centuries. The prophet Jeremiah inquired of the Lord, "if I argued my case with you, you would prove to be right, Yet, I must question you about matters of justice. Why are the wicked so prosperous?" (Jeremiah 12:1, GNT).

The Psalmist also asked why the wicked prospered, and he admitted being envious of them. Godliness did not seem to "pay off." Then the Lord revealed the wicked person's end—sudden eternal punishment.

> God is indeed good . . . to those who have pure hearts. But I had nearly lost confidence; my faith was almost gone because I was jealous of the proud when I saw that things go well for the wicked . . . I tried to think this problem through, but it was too difficult for me until I went into your Temple. Then I understood what will happen to the wicked. You will put them in slippery places and make them fall to destruction! They are instantly destroyed; they go down to a horrible end! (Psalm 73:1-3, 16-19, GNT).

The Bible tells us that some of the wicked will prosper, but it does not say why they prosper. However, what the Lord does tell us is not to worry. Do not envy the wicked person who prospers, because life on earth is so short that he will fade away quickly. ". . . Do not be provoked by evildoers; do not envy those who do wrong. Like grass they wither quickly; like green plants they wilt away" (Psalm 37:1-2). We are encouraged to maintain the Lord's eternal perspective with his eternal value system.

Question: What does the Bible say about lawsuits?

Answer: More than 22,000 civil lawsuits are filed each day in our nation! Unfortunately, many of these suits pit Christian against Christian at an annual cost of millions of dollars.

Suing seems to be a national pastime: A woman from Maryland sued a man who she said kicked her at a dance. She sought $200,000 as compensation for the injury and time lost on the dance floor. A former professional football player was awarded $300,000 for the "psychological injury" he suffered from being called a "chicken" by the team doctor.

There are a number of reasons for this flood of lawsuits, including an avalanche of new laws and regulations. More disturbing, people are becoming less and less forgiving.

The current court system uses an adversarial judicial process, which frequently creates animosities and fractures relationships between the parties involved. Instead of trying to heal the wounds, the system provides a technical and legal solution to the case but leaves the problems of a lack of forgiveness and anger untouched. The overriding objective in litigation is to win.

Yet the Bible stresses that the goal should be reconciliation. "If you are about to offer your gift to God at the altar and there you remember that your brother has something against you, leave your gift there in front of the altar, go at once and make peace with your brother . . . " (Matthew 5:23-24, GNT).

Scripture states clearly that when Christians are at odds with one another, they should not settle their disputes through the secular courts.

> If any of you have a dispute with another Christian, how dare you go before heathen judges instead of letting God's people settle the matter? Don't you know that God's people will judge the world? Well, then, if you are to judge the world, aren't you capable of judging small matters? Do you not know that we shall judge the angels? How much more, then, the things of this life! If such matters come up, are you going to take them to be settled by people who have no standing

in the church? Shame on you! Surely there is at least one wise person in your fellowship who can settle a dispute between fellow Christians. Instead, one Christian goes to court against another and lets unbelievers judge the case! The very fact you have legal disputes among yourselves shows you have failed completely. Would it not be better for you to be wronged? Would it not be better for you to be robbed? (1 Corinthians 6:1-7, GNT)

Instead of initiating a lawsuit, a three-step procedure for Christians to resolve their differences is set forth in Matthew 18:15-17 (GNT): "If your brother sins against you, go to him and show him his fault. But do it privately, just between yourselves. If he listens to you, you have won your brother back. But if he will not listen to you, take one or two other persons with you, so that 'every accusation may be upheld by the testimony of two or more witnesses.'"

1. Go in private. The party who believes he has been wronged needs to confront the other person in private with his claims. If the dispute remains unresolved, then . . .

2. Go with one or two others. The person who feels wronged should return with witnesses who can confirm facts or help resolve the dispute. If this is still unsuccessful, then . . .

3. Go before the church. The third step is mediation or arbitration before an impartial group in the church or perhaps a local Christian mediation service, if this is available in your area.

The greatest benefit of following this procedure is not simply reaching a fair settlement of the dispute, but practicing forgiveness, fostering peace and demonstrating love.

Question: What does the Lord say about favoritism (partiality)?

Answer: The Bible is clear. Carefully study James 2:1-9:

> My brothers, show no partiality as you adhere to the faith in our glorious Lord Jesus Christ. For if a man with gold rings on his fingers and in fine clothes comes into your assembly, and a poor person in shabby clothes also comes in, and you pay attention to the one wearing the fine clothes and say, "Sit here, please," while you say to the poor one, "Stand there," or "Sit at my feet," have you not made distinctions among yourselves and become judges with evil designs?

> Listen, my beloved brothers. Did not God choose those who are poor in the world to be rich in faith and heirs of the kingdom that he promised to those who love him? But you dishonored the poor person. Are not the rich oppressing you? And do they themselves not haul you off to court? Is it not they who blaspheme the noble name that was invoked over you? However, if you fulfill the royal law according to the scripture, "You shall love your neighbor as yourself," you are doing well. But if you show partiality, you commit sin, and are convicted by the law as transgressors.

I have struggled with the sin of partiality. I wouldn't be so obvious as to tell one to stand and another to sit in a favored place, but in my heart I have often been guilty of favoritism, and this has unintentionally influenced my actions. I know that I show partiality when I have preconceived notions about people. It's a constant battle for me to be aware of this.

Partiality does not have to be based solely on a person's wealth. It can also be based on a person's education, social position in the community or spiritual status in the church. James 2:9 could not be more direct: "But if you show partiality, you are committing sin and are convicted by the law as transgressors." How do we break the habit of partiality?

Romans 12:10 (GNT) tells us, "Love one another warmly as Christians, and be eager to show respect for one another." And Philippians 2:3 reads, "Do nothing out of selfishness or vainglory;

rather, humbly regard others as more important than yourselves." We need to ask the Lord to ingrain in our thinking the habit of elevating each person, regardless of his or her station in life, as more important than ourselves. One practical way to overcome partiality is to concentrate on the strengths and abilities of each person. Every person can do some things better than I can. This realization helps me appreciate all people.

Question: What does the Bible say about coveting?

Answer: Coveting means to desire or crave another person's property. Coveting is expressly prohibited throughout Scripture. The last two Commandments read, "You shall not covet your neighbor's house; you shall not covet your neighbor's wife, nor his male or his female slave, nor his ox or his ass nor anything that belongs to him" (Exodus 20:17). The commandments end with an infinitely broad prohibition: "or anything that belongs to him." In other words, we are commanded not to covet anything that belongs to anyone!

Greed is similar to coveting. "Since you are God's people, it is not right that any matters of sexual immorality or indecency or greed should even be mentioned amount you . . . You may be sure that no one who is immoral, indecent, or greedy (for greed is a form of idolatry) will ever receive a share in the Kingdom of Christ and of God" (Ephesians 5:3, 5; GNT).

A greedy or covetous person is an idolater. Coveting and greed have been called the universal, silent sins. Rarely are they addressed or confronted, but I believe they are among the most widespread sins of this generation. When I began studying what the Bible teaches about money, I was overwhelmed by the extent of my own coveting. Ask the Lord to show you if you are guilty of coveting that which is another's. If you are, repent and submit to the Holy Spirit. Ask him to change your heart.

Question: How much should we give and where should we give?

Answer: Once you have made the decision to give from your "first fruits" it is suggested that at least fifty percent of your gifts of time, talent and treasure, should go to your parish. The balance of your gifts should be split between other worthwhile religious, educational and charitable organizations. The Bishop's Annual Appeal or Diocesan Appeal should be considered when making gifts for the "other half" of your stewardship commitment. A general guideline for this appeal is one percent of your income.

Numerous secular charities (such a schools, fraternal orders or organizations formed to fight diseases) compete vigorously for our gift dollars. The Bible doesn't address whether or not we should give to these charities. However, Evelyn and I have decided not to normally support these organizations with our gifts. Our reason is that while many people support secular charities, only those who know the Lord support the ministries of Christ. We have occasionally given to secular charities when we sensed the Lord's prompting to give or when the solicitor was a friend we wanted to encourage or influence for Christ.

Question: The Scriptures repeatedly prohibit idolatry. How is that applicable in our modern age?

Answer: Few people today bow before stone pillars or golden statues. That form of idolatry is a thing of the past. However, we are always in danger of substituting other things in the place of God and of devoting to them the affection, which is due him alone. Practical idolatry is everywhere. As someone said, "Most idols today have four wheels, tinted glass, chrome and baked-on enamel." God should have first place in our hearts. His perspective should influence every decision we make. Everything should be subordinated to our love of him. If we love anything—family, job or possessions—more than the Lord, it is an idol.

ENDNOTES

1   Charles L. Allen, *God's Psychiatry* (Old Tappan, NJ: Revell, 1953)

2   David McConaughy, *Money, the Acid Test* (Philadelphia: Westminister Press, 1981), pp 24, 25

3   Herb Goldberg and Robert Lewis, *Money Madness* (New York: Morro, 1978), pp 13, 14

4   Randy Alcorn, *Money, Possessions and Eternity* (Carol Stream, IL: Tyndale House Publishers), pp. 128, 129.

5   George Fooshee, *You Can Be Financially Free* (Old Tappan, NJ: Revell, 1976), p26.

6   George Fooshee, *You Can Beat the Money Squeeze* (Fleming H Revell, 1980)

NOTES